MORE FAST FOOD FOR THE SOUL

11/25/07

Ronald Charles Lacy

Bite-size Servings of Hope and Inspiration

Donald Charles Lacy

Providence House Publishers

FRANKLIN, TENNESSEE

Printed in the United States of America

11   10   09   08   07   1   2   3   4   5

Library of Congress Control Number: 2007924435

ISBN: 978-1-57736-391-0

Cover illustration by Joey McNair
Cover and page design by Joey McNair

PROVIDENCE HOUSE PUBLISHERS
238 Seaboard Lane • Franklin, Tennessee 37067
www.providence-publishing.com
800-321-5692

To all those precious human beings who read this book,
I will be praying for your spiritual successes.

Preface

The reflections on contemporary issues found in *More Fast Food for the Soul* set up situations, then provide suggested solutions, often with a great deal of humor. The intent of the book is to have broad appeal to all age levels. I hope it will be a useful resource in many situations: during times of personal reflection, for use during public speaking engagements, for opening or closing meetings, as pastoral helps, or as a gift for graduates, family, friends, or co-workers.

I wrote a newspaper column for the *New Castle Courier-Times* for seven years. My first volume of columns, *Fast Food for the Soul*, was generally a popular Indiana and Midwest book. *More Fast Food for the Soul* is intended to be broader and more national in scope—plus all of the material is completely new.

In his foreword to the first volume, Darrell Radford, former managing editor of the *New Castle Courier-Times*, said, "The pieces don't take long to read but often stick with you like grandmother's cooking—nutritional morsels of spiritual truth presented in a nondenominational way."

I encourage you to grab some *More Fast Food* and enjoy the nourishing insights in this special collection.

—Donald Charles Lacy

MORE FAST FOOD FOR THE SOUL

"**I** could write a book," the pastor said with a certain finality that made you believe he would. His intention came out loud and clear, almost arrogantly.

He was in his fifties and had known many joys in the parish. He had also known his share of sorrows. In truth, his wisdom was obvious, but so were his battle scars.

Those who heard him make the remark knew a great deal about his life and the battles he had fought. Most were in sympathy. A few felt threatened by his tone.

Frankly, some even wondered if the time had come for him to tell the truth about people who had confided in him. There was an uneasiness. Maybe he would tell all! There were those who could visualize him authoring a best-selling novel that would contain shocking information and create a scandal.

Then came a time of "wait and see." Would it be published in a year or two? Would it take longer? Maybe it would never see print, but people would continue to speculate.

He had touched many lives and had been in the community several years. Generally, he was respected, but there were also those who saw it otherwise. Other pastors probably have had similar experiences. To be in the pastoral ministry is to know a lot about some people's lives, and also to experience hate and hurt.

Of course, such a novel would certainly carry with it joys and successes. Yet readers, it seems, are always more interested in the seamy side of things. That's what sells.

Would the pastor really write a book? In his heart and mind it finally came down to whether he would yield to temptation. Some days he could picture the people and their naughty ways in print.

He wasn't much of a writer, but he knew that didn't really matter. There were ghostwriters around who could craft fine paragraphs, and they knew how to incite readers.

The struggle went on and the people waited. He could sense a justice in all of this and a chance to make things right. The years passed, yet no book appeared. Following the pastor's death, his private papers were reviewed, but nothing scandalous was found. However, they did find a book title, followed by four words: "May God be merciful."

2   A Clash of Generations

"Marriage is not an experiment," the grandmother rather bluntly told her granddaughter. There was authority in the elderly lady's voice. You couldn't miss her firmness.

The young woman wanted to experiment with a so-called trial marriage. The plan was simple. She and her boyfriend would live together for a year and then decide about marriage. After all, she was only twenty-four years old and had a good job. It appeared to be a promising arrangement.

Well, her grandmother complicated the matter by inquiring about her previous living-together arrangement with a different young man. Grandmother reminded her that life was moving along faster than the young woman realized. How many more experiments would there be?

The scene became tense. This wasn't what the young woman wanted to hear. She was even so bold as to tell her grandmother she would have been better off doing some experimenting. In her opinion, Grandfather was no prize.

Grandmother was married at the age of seventeen, and had three children by the time she was twenty-four. She put a priority on being a good mother and grandmother. In fact, she couldn't think of anything more important.

There had been only one man in her life that mattered, and she married him. This was no trial-and-error experiment. It was for a lifetime.

She was really concerned about the pattern her granddaughter seemed to be developing. How could this ever lead her to happiness? Surely God expected more—a lot more. Grandmother not only found the younger woman's outlook absurd, but outright sinful. The granddaughter found that point of view hilarious. God didn't punish people for sex outside of marriage.

Is the grandmother old-fashioned and unrealistic? Doesn't she believe in equality of the sexes? "Men are men, and it's best to find out all you can about them before you settle for one," her granddaughter demanded.

Despite their opposing viewpoints, they never stopped loving one another. The granddaughter promised to step back and take another look at her life. There was hope.

3   It's All in the Focusing

"**D**on't bother me," Dad said to his six-year-old son. A work project had to be completed and it was due within hours. Of course, the youngster didn't understand.

Mom was less than understanding and let it be known. Surely there was time for their son. They weren't together that often and needed to be.

In fact, she began to accuse her husband of being uncaring and even heartless. She saw a little boy yearning for his father's undivided attention. Painful situation.

Dad already felt sorry about it, and more blame was the last thing he needed. He began to seethe beneath the surface. He had no answer except to go on concentrating.

The little fellow became more insistent, especially with his mother's prodding. It seemed to be a no-win situation, and the tension increased minute by minute.

Finally, Dad stopped what he was doing and peered out the window. He prayed in unspoken words that somehow and someway a solution could be found. He would not erupt in anger.

His time of brief pondering made him review his responsibility to God, family, and job. He really wanted to be good at meeting all expectations. Then a divine light bulb came on.

He took his son and put him on his lap. Then he slipped his computer and other work-related items to one side. It was time for fatherly goodness and gentle firmness.

In a few moments—by the grace of God—he communicated a loving attitude with kind words and delightful hugs. His son was wanted. A son is a son and that's important.

Surprisingly, after about five minutes, the boy got off his father's lap with confidence and went joyfully about other things.

Even Mom was surprised but elated. She wanted to applaud but decided just maybe that would be a little too much. So much was accomplished in such a short time.

Concentration was the key. While his project demanded absolute focus, so did those tender moments with his son. His son needed to have his full attention, regardless of the time span.

So, whether we are dealing with cold facts and figures or relating to our children or other adults, we must be totally interested to be victorious. Remember to stay focused.

4   We Are to Smell the Roses

"Take time to smell the roses along the way," a mother told her ambitious son. I guess most of us know what she meant, but he didn't at the time. It took a while for him to learn.

He was in his late teens and had plans to revolutionize this world—if not the next. Why bother with her outdated advice? It didn't mean anything.

To be fair he was a fine, intelligent lad. He simply didn't want anyone to get in his way. He knew he could be anything he wanted to be, and he intended to set his own pace.

He loved his mother, but she seemed to get too sentimental. She also talked about things in a way that didn't seem to help anymore. But he knew that wasn't her fault.

His life and career moved along at a blistering speed. People noticed and admired him. Noteworthy accomplishments were common.

Mothers have a way of placing things in your mind that you will remember. Once in a while he would think about smelling the roses. Roses are beautiful flowers. The colors, shades, and varieties seem unlimited. A dozen red roses given to a special person is very precious.

He would then chuckle at himself for pausing to consider roses.

Life continued at a breakneck pace. There were defeats now and then, but they were temporary setbacks. He was really making something of himself.

He was out of the country when his mother died. He made it back in time for the funeral with only minutes to spare. The organist was already playing the final song.

He moved to view her corpse with profound gratitude and the sadness of her passing. On her casket were dozens of red roses.

He was mesmerized by the sight, and tears came for the first time in years. He had not had time to cry before now, only to succeed as the world measures success. He was embarrassed because he could not hold back the tears.

His younger sister came to stand with him, and gently touched his shoulder. He had not seen her for many years.

Mom had known what she was talking about; for the first time he was ready to pay attention. Some things would have to wait. It was time to smell the roses.

5   Integrating God's Word

"Live victoriously," Aunt Sally always maintained. Throughout her life she said that to everyone she met. Some were a bit embarrassed when she said it, but no one said so.

She was now in her later years and must have shared that advice thousands of times. When people saw her, those words came to mind and they usually just smiled. Her influence was obvious.

No one had ever really asked her why she said what she did. The simple assumption was that she was a very religious lady. That was as far as it went.

Aunt Sally was humble and enthusiastic. In many ways she was a model of the power of positive thinking—and more. Her confidence never left her and it seemed to be a gift of God.

At last, curiosity got the best of one man. He approached her at a small informal gathering to ask her reason for proclaiming that motto.

Her answer was mostly scriptural. She began with: "My grace is sufficient for you, for my power is made perfect in weakness" (2 Cor. 12:9 RSV).

Then, she moved to: "Have no anxiety about anything, but in everything by prayer and supplication with thanksgiving let your requests be made known to God" (Phil. 4:6 RSV).

She stopped speaking and a big smile came to her face. She quickly quoted, "And the peace of God, which passes all understanding, will keep your hearts and your minds in Christ Jesus" (Phil. 4:7 RSV).

But she wasn't finished yet. She spoke very carefully, "Love is patient and kind; it is not jealous or conceited or proud" (1 Cor. 13:4 TEV).

Many around her put their heads down. By now some were beginning to understand. She still wasn't through. With uplifted voice she proclaimed, "I have the strength to face all conditions by the power that Christ gives me" (Phil. 4:13 TEV).

Everyone was listening intently as she indicated there was more: "Be joyful always, pray at all times, be thankful in all circumstances" (1 Thess. 5:16–18 TEV).

Aunt Sally quoted each Scripture from memory. In truth, they were said every day . . . many times. She had more to say, however, that was quite enough for the moment. Living victoriously took on a meaning that made it wonderfully reachable. The Scripture had been integrated into her life.

What have you and I integrated into our lives?

Intellectuals Need Love, Too

"**N**ot enough love in this world," bemoaned the learned old fellow. He was a retired college professor. Philosophy and the social sciences were his major fields, and he delved a bit into theology.

For all of his years of accomplishment and satisfaction, one thing remained. There was this elusive quality called love, especially in the Christian sense. His yearning was noticeable.

He had climbed the heights with Socrates, Plato, and Aristotle. People like Thomas Aquinas and Francis Bacon thrilled him. Yes, there were Rousseau, Spinoza, and many others.

It had been such a wonderful life in academia, except that he never seemed to find an unconditional love. To be sure, he loved his teaching. Often the students were challenging.

Yet, in retirement he languished in a struggle that seemed to tear at his heart over and over. All that he knew and felt never quite got him to where he really wanted to be.

The crucifixion and resurrection story was always interesting but it had no more impact than other stories coming from religions. After all, wasn't one as good as the other? He had long held this view.

He had days at a time to reflect on his upbringing. His father had been a stern Lutheran and his mother an Independent Baptist. The two never talked much about religion.

Early on, he had more or less shelved both and sought to live his life in a moral fashion. Jesus was one of his beacons but only one among several. He did not want to be confined by the teachings of any one sect.

Then, it happened! He realized something he had missed all along. This love for which he was searching was much closer than he thought. His parents both found love in Jesus.

Like a child, now teachable, the holy rays of grace came upon the retired professor. He knew now that a solitary man had willingly given all He had for him. His death was really a sacrifice for all.

He pondered the horrors of the crucifixion. He discovered there was probably no other death so humiliating and excruciating. Jesus had done nothing wrong and His purity was well known.

That was the love for which he was looking. Away with perfect philosophical systems and social engineering. Away with theological language that had no flesh and blood. Peace at last.

So, the crucifixion of Jesus Christ became more than another story to tell. It became a living reality in his life. This led to the professor's rebirth and a love that knows no bounds.

7   A Larger Picture of Love

"Love me or leave me," she blurted out to her husband. It was not a pleasant scene. So much seemed to be falling apart in their marriage and the sparks were flying.

There were many factors. Some that were the most important simply had to do with what love was all about. Their definitions often seemed to contradict.

For her, they must be together on all occasions, except when they went to work. So, when she went to visit her family, he also needed to go. Togetherness was a major sign of love for the woman.

Her husband didn't feel that had much to do with love. In fact, when she went to see her parents, he set out for the lake to go fishing. This really upset her.

Then, there was her need for gifts to express his love. Wasn't she worth it? After all, she was his wife and other husbands found ways to come home with flowers, candy, etc.

He did remember the special days like her birthday, Christmas, and their anniversary, but that wasn't enough. When she had a tough day at work, something from him would have helped.

For him, their bedroom time meant faithfulness most of all. She was his wife and he would never stray from her. Of course, he didn't say that to her very often.

She admitted he cared for her but not in ways she expected. Their private lives, especially that which involved lovemaking, didn't mean much to her. Her husband seemed totally self-absorbed and little interested in her enjoyment.

How long was she supposed to wait before he got the message? She'd had enough. For the most part, her needs were not being met and she was going to do something about it. Either he would change or he could be on his way elsewhere. Yes, it was time for him to "shape up or ship out."

Is there a way to keep them together? Is this situation as one-sided as it appears to be? Why wasn't all of this addressed in pre-marital counseling?

It's unlikely this young man will ever be able to give his wife all the attention she craves. Who can really blame him? However, he needs to try to be more loving in the ways that have value to her.

Attention and recognition are often needs that mask other problems. Perhaps both have not accepted the fact that all true love and worth come from God. Apart from God, love can become a manipulative game.

8   Differences Need Not Be Divisive

"**I**'m getting married!" she joyfully exclaimed. Everyone around her was also thrilled. It was an occasion of celebration for all concerned, all except for Uncle Bill.

He thought she was marrying the wrong man, and he said so. His reasons were simple and direct. Her husband expected her to work after she was married and there would be no children for five years.

Uncle Bill was having a hard time with that. He came from the old school that mandated the man is to be the provider if at all possible. And a major reason for getting married is to have children.

These ideas were so foreign to the future bride's way of thinking that she secretly laughed behind her uncle's back. The poor man was so out of touch with the real world, it's best he be ignored.

Well, Bill had just turned eighty. He had spent three years serving in World War II, and was a survivor of the Battle of the Bulge. God had protected him all the way.

He was a grateful man with great wisdom. He was not a bigot in any area of his life. Her uncle was good natured and attended church faithfully.

It just made sense to him that manhood involved providing for one's wife and family. Drawing together in holy wedlock was filled with hope because children would soon be on the way.

Nevertheless, the young couple had worked out their arrangement about jobs and children. They were not about to be swayed by anyone, including Uncle Bill. In their minds, all was settled.

The clash of values between generations is an ever-present force. It takes tolerance and a willingness to adjust to the day and time in which we live. It also takes gratitude for the sacrifices of other generations.

Having witnessed these differences numerous times while serving in the church, I have been careful to listen and then recommend. There is certainly a movement away from the biblical viewpoints that men are to provide for their wives and families, and every couple is supposed to be blessed by having children.

But let's not come down too hard on either side. Women have always worked, and many for very little or no financial reward. And in this case, the couple has not ruled out having children in the future.

Bigger questions remain: Is their proposed style of living one that will keep their marriage intact? Will it be one filled with love, respect, and trust?

If those are answered yes, then I believe Uncle Bill will give his blessing.

9 ## Fathers Are Not Replaceable

"I miss my daddy," the little guy said with big tears in his eyes. He was in the first grade and his life had been shattered. Divorce was taking its toll in heartbreaking ways.

He used to see his daddy every night before he went to bed and many other times as well. Not so anymore. The terms of the divorce were such that every other weekend would be the pattern for visitation.

The reasons for the marital breakup were several in number. The reality was there was a broken home and a little boy's heart ripped apart. Sometimes he cried into the night.

His father and mother just couldn't make it. At least, that is what they thought. After all, wasn't it better to divorce, remarry, and have peace than fight all the time?

Such reasoning, careful though it may be, has never carried much weight with me. For one thing, there is a false assumption. In short, how do you know a second marriage will be an improvement?

Who is going to mend that little boy's heart? Will a new daddy suffice? We all know the answer to that one and we are prone to hide our heads in the sand.

Sometimes when I see children wanting their daddies, I cry too. I plead with God to give us a better way of handling our big problems.

"Father hunger" is a term used to describe much of what is going on today. In a profound way this is also God hunger. The Scriptures over and over call God the Father.

Jesus cried out to His Father. Little children cry out for their fathers. There is a mysterious relationship in all of this and it goes into the depths of who and what we really are.

Despite the so-called enlightened attempts of some cultural engineers, the need for fathers in the traditional sense never goes away. When they are absent, we cry out for them.

As perhaps never before, boys and girls need to identify with their fathers. How else can they begin to know who and what they are? The enormity of our failures is ever before us.

Remember this, dads: Once a father, always a father (unless you deliberately refuse your rightful place). No one on the face of this earth can take fatherhood from you—except you.

Now, wipe the tears from your children's eyes and tell them how much you love them. Then hug them until they say that's enough. There is no replacement for good fathers.

Gender Differences Are Always With Us

"Off to his cave," the young wife said in exasperation. They had had another argument and conflict ensued.

Tension had been building and she had just tried her usual solution. She wanted to talk it out right away. She reasoned if they could just talk for a time, all would be well. It seemed so simple to her. After all, they had been husband and wife for more than three years. Surely they were mature enough to settle this dispute by talking? So, she began more or less a barrage of words.

As usual, her husband said very little, then left in his car. He drove down the highway to a city several miles away and found a restaurant in which to plant himself.

In fact, he planted himself for more than two hours. He drank coffee and tried to figure out what had happened . . . again. His wife wanted to talk, but he needed time in his cave to think through the situation and come up with a solution.

When he was sure he had a solution, he returned home . . . very late. As he entered the house, he saw his wife waiting for him. He started to tell her how he had reasoned through their predicament and had come up with an answer.

However, she began by telling him what a bum he was and that she suspected he was with another woman. She berated him in unpleasant and uncomplimentary terms.

As usual, he sat there with his mouth open. He couldn't believe what he was hearing!

His wife began to cry. She honestly did not understand why he didn't stay home for them to talk it out. That was how she'd resolve it. But he was different. He just couldn't react that way.

Why does a man have to run off to his cave? Why does a woman have to settle the difficulty with many words? Generally, it's the difference in communication styles between the two genders.

And so, it often is that way in married life. Husbands and wives have different ways of handling their disagreements. We clergy discover this situation to be commonplace.

When couples come to me, I usually explain to the wife that her husband hasn't stopped loving her and he cares for her deeply. I then tell the husband to call his wife from his cave, giving her his exact location.

11   Our Blessed Lord Knows Best

"I don't know what to do," his wife said under her breath. Her husband was being humiliated and he didn't even know it. She was suffering more pain every moment.

It was a company party and she was several feet away from her husband. At least a half dozen people stood between them. Her husband was unaware that in the center of his back had been placed a sticker saying, "I can't stand Big Name University."

It seemed like a practical joke—until one realized the event. Management had gathered to celebrate a lucrative contract signing with none other than Big Name University.

Most everyone had seen the sticker, and his wife was dying little by little. But he just kept talking away, seeming to have the time of his life. He had a little too much alcohol to drink, and that didn't help at all.

To make matters even worse, the person representing the university was very sensitive. Practical jokes were OK—unless you were poking fun at something he considered sacred.

There must be some way to rescue the poor fellow. Maybe it wasn't too late. His wife hoped it would not cost him his job.

Sometimes, however, little affronts at big parties do cost jobs in the long run. Those who have been in situations that involved position and power know the dynamics. Sometimes human egos are very fragile, even in high places.

The pride that is in all of us can sometimes control our best impulses. When we feel offended or slighted, we can become hateful.

Why some respond this way, I don't know. I like to give everyone the benefit of the doubt and believe we can all overcome a slight or mistake here and there.

Some years ago, I remember the trustee of a major university telling a coach to eat a piece of cake prepared by the influential hostess. The coach tried to decline in a mannerly way.

The trustee kept insisting, and the scene became ugly. It was obvious the dessert would be eaten or the coach would have to find another place of employment. It was a very sad day.

Why are power, pride, position, and prestige so important? Some say that's just the way it is in the real world.

What if our Blessed Lord had said that's just the way it is in the real world, and left us to our own devices?

12 Christians Are Intended to Enjoy Each Other

"Across the divide," the pastor said with a highly noticeable twinkle in his eye. What did he mean? The others present soon learned it was that ecumenical thing about Christians working together.

Several prominent clergy and laity from area churches had gathered—something they really hadn't done together. It seems each was content to do the denominational thing. There was, frankly, a lot of competition for new members or converts.

They seemed to be comfortable with that style. After all, "You do your thing and I'll do my thing. Christ will still be glorified." We don't need to mingle—except in the workplace, the sports events, and virtually everyplace else.

Well, the pastor with the twinkle in his eye showed those gathered very clearly that it just made sense to cross the divide now and then. He began to point out there was so much more that we shared than what divided us. Surely God's people could learn from one another.

Everyone at the meeting was well-mannered and kind. But something became quite clear to those who were more perceptive. Regardless of the common bond of God's Spirit among them, they preferred things to stay the way they were.

Oh, maybe we can play at church cooperation by physically being around one another—as long as we don't change. The game is all right and it gives the public a positive feeling.

I am sometimes amazed by well-meaning people who profess Christ and yet don't want anything to do with those outside their group. The call to Christians has always been to be one under Christ. Why, then, does segregation occur among denominations?

This may sound old-fashioned or inadequate, but I believe the devil continually works at keeping us separated.

Those who have served as missionaries in foreign countries tell me they don't have time for denominationalism. If they took the time to be separate, they would be doomed to failure.

I began my career as a public school teacher in Jay County, Indiana. I have loved to teach and learn all my life. Religiously speaking, some of the best learning is done among those who are different.

What does a United Methodist know about a Lutheran? It is time to learn. What does a Presbyterian know about a Catholic? It is time to learn. On and on the list goes.

Why refuse to be enriched and nurtured by those who love the Lord under a different label? To miss those opportunities makes no sense. We can all do better.

13   Loosen Up and Admire These Women

"True blue," the plant supervisor responded, when asked about a certain employee. The person in question was a young, single mother with five children.

She worked her forty-hour week plus all the overtime she could get, so her paychecks were as big as she could possibly make them. Her children had clothes and did not go hungry.

Her dedication to both her job and her children were obvious to anyone who was interested in the facts. Of course, not everyone is all that interested in facts, so a problem emerged.

Rumors were floating around about her sub-par care for her children. Someone also managed to start a rumor about her being too familiar with some men.

There were even those who seemed to think she was not doing her job well. There was all this and more, too. Obviously someone wanted to hurt this young woman.

From the viewpoint of those who really knew her, all that was outright injustice. She was a good woman living under difficult circumstances.

What makes some people want to destroy an individual who is faithful in every aspect of her life? In this case, a man and a woman were the culprits.

The man just didn't believe a woman with small children should be working all those hours away from them.

What he didn't understand was that she had to. By working and providing for her children, she avoided welfare. All she had was her job, children, and church. She never spent time any other place.

The critical woman worked near the young mother and noticed the looks she occasionally got from men.

What this critic didn't understand was the young lady had no interest in men. Remarriage at this point in her life was unthinkable. She never flirted.

When our ideas about how life is to be lived become too rigid, we often fail to allow for exceptions. This young mother was an exception, and at least two people didn't like it.

I marvel at those young, single women who are so faithful to the highest and best we know. There are traps of various kinds all around them, yet they stay the course.

Please take a moment to affirm and admire those who refuse to be compromised. There is a bit of saintliness in them. We must pray for them and hope for their futures.

"Deliver the goods or else," a gruff boss told his employee. The message was direct and clear. A certain prescribed job had to be done or the fellow had to leave.

This has always been true in the work-a-day world. Oh, we have phrased the words differently, but the message is the same. An employee either does his or her job, or leaves.

Now, all of this sounds simple enough. Either we or someone we know has been there and done that, sometimes more than once.

Yet I don't think it's really all that simple. People get fired for failing to deliver the goods. What exactly are the goods, and who defines the conditions of employment?

You and I both know it is frequently the intangibles, things that really cannot be measured, that carry the real weight. After all, what really is a job description?

I have seen the pages, long and detailed, in language everyone seems to understand. Some of them are even laid out very attractively. But the job description is not really the job—and what's expected of an employee is frequently not expressed in that written document.

Over the years, I have spoken with a number of persons who were let go but didn't know why. They had delivered the goods as they understood them. That apparently wasn't enough.

I remember a fellow in his fifties who had been around the block enough times to develop a realistic approach to this. When he was handed a job description, he made an inquiry.

He would look into the eyes of his potential employer and say, "I can read but what do you really expect?" Now, that's applied wisdom in a real world.

It's quite possible to check off everything expected of you with dispatch. Will that keep you employed? Well, the answer, as you may have guessed, is no. In an imperfect world, with the unpredictability of human relations, that's just the way things are. (Share this bit of insight with your sons and daughters. They need to know.)

In one of my parishes, I was expected to preach good sermons, administer the affairs of the church, and visit the sick. At least, that's what the official committee told me.

Boy, was I in for a rude awakening. They failed to point out a major human relations assignment: I had to get along with Aunt Sadie, come hell or high water. I left after one year.

15   Consult God's Will and Ways

"The guy isn't content anywhere," his wife related with a tone of concern. Her husband couldn't seem to find himself. He had given up some good-paying jobs.

A few months here and a few months there had been his pattern for a long time. His family had become unhappy. When was Dad going to land for a while?

I guess we have all known these people. Some of them are talented and not afraid to apply themselves at work. At the same time, however, something just doesn't quite click in their lives.

One of the best examples I can remember was a fellow in seminary. His story may not be that unusual. He was in mid-life and had already worked a number of jobs.

With blunt honesty, he revealed that one day he finally recognized his problem. God had called him into the ordained ministry but he kept running away. Eventually, he said, "Yes, Lord."

One time he told me that if God would just leave him alone and not make him be a minister, he would go out and make a million dollars. He'd be a success.

God didn't leave him alone. He learned that, one way or another, God always wins.

Many people are coming into the ordained ministry in mid-life. I believe they are doing so for the right reasons and they appear to be content.

Are you where you belong in life? Perhaps a better question is, "Do you sense you are where God wants you?" Life is too short to wander about in discontentment.

I really loved teaching history and English, but that was not what God wanted. I really wanted to be an attorney with a political career, but that was not what God wanted either.

For the sake of your souls here and now, yes, and forever, be sure you are where God wants you. It is no secret what He can do for you. He can put at rest all your wandering.

Contentment does not have to rob you of your creativity. There is a peace that passes all understanding. Only the God who created you can provide that.

My pilgrimage tells me the Creator is always a perfect blend of love and justice. That is not to imply it all happens in this life. In fact, I am fairly certain it doesn't.

I close with a simple suggestion. Find a quiet corner in your world and meditate on a few simple words with all your heart: "Here I am, Lord; I am ready to go where You lead me."

16 The Awesome Power of God's Spirit

"The wind blows where it blows," a pensive young woman said softly. She was sitting in her backyard and a breeze gave her a sense of well being yet mystery. It was a mystical moment.

She was thinking about life and death. For some reason they seemed closer than ever before. There was something about the awesomeness of the wind. God was present.

In time she came to a comparison of it and the Holy Spirit. It came to her that no one really controls the wind. A person may work using it, but no one controls the wind. Likewise the Holy Spirit cannot be controlled at all. The Holy Spirit moves where He wants, blows where He blows.

The Holy Scriptures speak often about this Spirit. Through the centuries, serious-minded Christians have had difficulty relating to this God-given Spirit, and have even argued over definitions. Some, wrongly motivated, even tried to buy it.

Well, how about you and me? If asked, could we define it? I confess to you that I am a mere student in the study of the Holy Spirit. Yet, as I trace my steps back more than sixty years, His reality is there. This Holy Wind was much present throughout my life.

A basic understanding of the Christian faith says God chooses to come to us as Father, Son, and Holy Spirit. Understanding the concepts of Father and Son comes pretty easy, but how about the Holy Spirit?

Maybe God saw in humanity this craving to define and understand everything carefully and completely. Perhaps He sent the Holy Spirit—a force we cannot capture or fully comprehend—as a means to fill us with wonder, humble us, and keep us in our place.

Please do not infer that I mean an inferior place, because this never happens to God's children. Being human and incomplete, we must be humble to learn. That's the long and short of it.

I count on the Holy Spirit every moment of my life. I begin most days with this prayer: "May the fruit of the Holy Spirit be in evidence as I seek to fulfill my calling this day." This works.

When a gentle breeze touches your cheek or a heavy wind almost knocks you over, give thanks, for this is a reminder of God's gift to Christians. The Holy Spirit abides, provides, and guides.

17   Better Take Another Look

"Oh, kick him in the seat of the pants," the old codger shouted. The young fellow didn't want to carry his share of the load. The much older man was incensed and loud.

Those of us who grew up in a time when boys had certain rites of passage know exactly what this is all about. To become a man meant to work. Sometimes work wasn't very comfortable.

In teaching us to work, fathers and grandfathers could seem to be devoid of patience. To be lazy was often considered worse than breaching the Ten Commandments. It was probably easier to talk to God than to Dad.

But, as most of us know, the point was not to be cruel. Someday this twelve-year-old will need to support his wife and family. They will count on him.

Now, friends, times have changed, and in some cases they have changed a lot. I suppose today the punishments we received might be considered child abuse. Tough males probably did need to soften their ways.

I must admit to you, though, every young man I ever knew who got kicked in the seat benefitted from it. There was something about a strong male word (and hand) that helped.

I'll grant you there were those daddies and granddaddies who didn't have much use for feelings, yet I also suspect we are too feeling-oriented today. (Think about that for a couple of days.)

Have we lost something? Often today men have help from their wives in supporting the family. I think that is positive and yet I do wonder at times.

There was this thing about responsibility being fixed on the husband and father. That was the expectation and usually the reality. Any man who didn't support his wife and family was a bum.

I have seen this a harsh reality, mostly two generations ago. Things are easier now physically, but what about in other ways? Are men and women both better off today than fifty or sixty years ago?

Abortion, divorce, and drugs tell me we may be living in a time of serious decline in regard to human character. Is it possible character doesn't develop because we don't challenge behaviors for fear of hurting someone's feelings?

I hope you won't think I want to return to the "good old days." (They probably were not that good.) But folks, something is noticeably missing in today's families. Frankly, I doubt there is any real substitute for male authority and responsibility. To be a man in a serious sense includes both.

"**D**on't break his spirit," the old fellow said with emphasis. His hair was white and he was past eighty. You could tell he was a man who had experienced a lot in his life.

More pointedly, he was speaking about his grandson. There was real concern in his voice. His namesake was up against some really tough odds in unexpected places. Although he was physically miles away, in spirit he was on his knees with his grandson.

Newly graduated from theological seminary, his grandson was serving in his first full-time church position. The first few months all went well, even beyond his expectations.

Then, it seemed as if the bottom fell out. Some members began to find fault with this or that. Soon they reminded him that they paid his salary.

At first, he just sloughed it off. After all, he knew he couldn't please everybody all the time. They were good people and he had an awful lot to learn.

Much to his dismay, however, what he thought to be a passing condition was not. His job was threatened. In some minds, he just wasn't doing what he was supposed to do — he didn't conform to their ideas of what a minister should do or how he should act.

All of the pressure began to take its toll. He began to lose some of his confidence. The glow of early successes had begun to fade away.

His wife began to stay home from church activities. She not only wanted to leave the church, she wanted him out of the ministry. Pressure kept building and the word was out that he would soon be given a severance pay. He would have to find another church. By this time, he was driven to his knees with disillusionment and despair. Surely the dear Lord didn't want it this way and things could still change.

Maybe the ministry really wasn't for him after all. If he stayed in the ministry, would he lose his wife and baby girl? Would God forgive someone who walked away from a calling?

The words "My grace is sufficient for you, for my power is made perfect in weakness" (2 Cor. 12:9 NIV) came to him. He knew he would continue his ministry.

He called to tell his grandfather, but Grandfather already knew.

19 — So the Lottery Might Not Be the Answer

"If we could only win the lottery," she said again and again. Bills were piling up and their credit cards had almost reached their limits. Their finances were in poor shape.

She was still in her thirties and her husband was slightly older. They had moderately well-paying jobs and two children, ages eight and fourteen.

They did not think they were extravagant spenders in any way. Yet, they seemed to be losing ground daily in their financial world. The wife believed a quick win of substantial money would fix things.

Her husband wasn't so sure of this plan, but he went along with it anyway. For quite some time, they set aside a few dollars every week to buy lottery tickets.

Well, I am not one to come down for or against playing the lottery. After all, we believe in freedom of choice in America. That's simple enough.

Why should anyone get in the way of the excitement of a possible really big win? We all like to win. Frankly, when the Cubs win, I am on cloud nine.

Like all that pertains to good living, however, we have to get below the surface level and ask some hard questions. Would fifty dollars a month in lottery tickets buy other necessities, like school clothes?

Let's pursue the matter further. Will five hundred or six hundred dollars a year spent on lottery tickets make a house payment?

Are you getting the feeling I'm not as sold on the value of a lottery?

Then, just maybe, you are ready to tell me the successor to Judas Iscariot was chosen by lot. Of course, you would be right, and the Scriptures tell us two men were proposed. Matthias won.

So is playing the lottery a scriptural matter or not? Can we be good Christians and still play the lottery? What do you think?

In a much bigger picture, isn't all of life a stewardship? We are given time, energy, skills, and opportunities. I believe God will hold us accountable. I would hate to stand before the living God on judgment day and admit I preferred the lottery over a church budget.

20   Reading Scripture Carefully

"Give me liberty or give me death!" the great orator Patrick Henry proclaimed. His powerful speech made it possible for the raising of the militia.

Only recently did I learn that momentous speech of March 23, 1775, was given in a church. It was in Saint John's Episcopal Church in Richmond, Virginia. The

Second Virginia Convention met there during that week. I wish I could have been there!

I visited there during vacation recently and studied that sacred spot. It is hallowed ground and really one can only look in gratitude. The dear Lord must have seen fit on that special day to put religion and politics together.

It was but a mere moment in history when this happened, yet the whole course of humanity was changed.

Indeed, as one studies history, it's apparent much has hinged on a brief happening. Truly God was present!

I sometimes wonder how many times individuals have said under their breaths, "It's either freedom or the grave." Press the matter in your own life. When you reach the point where you must have freedom over any other concern, then it's an exciting trip.

People often quote the Scripture that knowing the truth will set you free (John 8:32). The funny thing is, many seldom refer to the verse immediately before that. It changes the context.

You see, verse thirty-one says we must obey Jesus' teachings and be His disciples. Taken together, this simply means we must be seriously Christian in order to know the truth and be set free.

Be sure to read the Gospel of John 8:31–32. It may give you a whole different point of view of freedom.

Truth, freedom, and death are linked together throughout our lives. I believe all great men and women know this. They also know freedom worth the name is costly.

The American Revolution meant pain, suffering, and death for brave men. This was a preliminary to the formulation of a great nation. Then, freedom could prevail.

Spiritually speaking, the free person is the one who dies daily and carries his or her cross. In a way, all of this is a fascinating enigma. Accept it, know the truth, and be set free.

Joseph Was Not a Miscellaneous Item

"**H**e didn't count," responded little Cindy to her Sunday school teacher. The class was talking about the birth of Jesus and the Christmas story. The name of Joseph came up.

Much time had been spent talking about God's Son and His mother, Mary. The children had even guessed how much Jesus weighed at birth. They mused Mary must have been beautiful.

So, where does this fellow, Joseph, fit in? Cindy gave an answer that made sense. He wasn't Jesus' real father because, after all, His mother conceived through the Holy Spirit.

Maybe he was just put in the story because every child needed a daddy everyone could see. It was a matter of tacking on a name, so Jesus and Mary wouldn't be embarrassed.

I suppose this may sound a little far-fetched to you. If it does, look at it in the light of today's society. Do fathers count, or are they simply for show?

Some fathers feel that way. I have conversed with those who feel like miscellaneous baggage. Mom has a good job but Dad isn't sure what his role is.

Such men believe they have no real place in the family, except to be seen at the right time. They may feel that all the needs of the family are already met. It can be a lonely and unsettling place.

Maybe Joseph felt like that. Mary and Jesus got all the attention. Yet, he did stick around and provide major assistance. The life-saving trip to Egypt was a good example.

For generations fathers have found their identity and usefulness primarily as breadwinners who provided financially for their families.

Now, after years of political, social, and economic change, their place has changed. Sometimes the father isn't the breadwinner; sometimes fathers don't seem to contribute anything to the family.

But take heart, there is a positive side. With this change comes a new freedom. Men have been given the chance to see they are worth more than the incomes they provide.

In fact, many fathers are in direct contact with their children—raising them—in ways that their fathers and grandfathers were not. Men are discovering new ways of counting for something.

So, you see, the genius of God the Father is unending. The future is not completely clear for today's fathers, but all we need to know is our Heavenly Father is at work— and that's what matters most.

22 Seldom Enough Time

"Call me any time, day or night," the young salesman said. He was serious and sincere. He was ambitious and wanted to do the very best for his company and himself.

As some of us with a little more experience know, he had opened himself to a parade of phone calls. Some were placed by people interested in his product; others simply called to visit or argue.

How accessible can we afford to be? For the pastor (no matter which denomination), that question is timely, and sooner or later has to be answered.

I have a lot of respect for my colleagues in ministry, especially those pastoring churches. It is a singular honor to be called of God to enter the ordained ministry, which also holds unique frustrations.

We all have somewhat different styles, but I will tell you how I handle those needing access to me. This is a plan that has remained fairly constant in recent years.

The weekday morning hours are spent in my church office, almost always with the door open. Generally, persons walk in or out at will. Of course, basic administration goes on.

The weekday afternoons are spent visiting in the parish area. This is not limited to residences. I often experience chance meetings in the community that benefit the church in different ways.

The weekday evenings are given to various meetings, whether they may be administrative, programmatic, or social in nature. Occasionally, an evening is free.

Saturdays are often filled with study sessions and weddings, plus pulling together loose ends for Sundays. I have learned, however, that to work all day Saturday is to be not fresh for Sunday!

So, how accessible can pastors be? It is not easy to tell someone standing in your office that you have to leave to go to a funeral home, especially if the person wasn't finished talking.

We all survive by the grace of God. At times, one of the wonders of life is that we pastors survive at all. Pastors are perhaps the most vulnerable species remaining on our planet.

Regardless, pastors really have to be accessible both day and night. Human need never ceases and a pastoral touch may be exactly what is required at a given time.

If a precious child of God calls at two o'clock in the morning and you have a six o'clock breakfast, you must listen and perhaps advise. The caller probably doesn't need theological expertise, just a friendly, caring voice.

Don't Cherish Bitterness

"**B**e careful with my husband; he is so bitter," the wife said. I suppose every adult can relate to that warning. Bitter people cause us discomfort, and frequently, pain.

Some people have lived with their bitterness so long they appear to be consumed by it. It shows in their faces, it even shows in the movements of their bodies. Everyone can see it.

What can really be done to help them? That's a very large order and some may be tempted to just say *forget it.*

I don't think that's a good option. Now, I am intelligent enough to know we might just be considered unwanted meddlers if we try to help. Yet I believe there is a helpful middle ground that could be considered.

I call this middle ground "a willingness to absorb bitterness and label it by its correct name."

The bitter person is someone who refuses to alter his or her understanding of life. In short, past bitter experience is encased in steel and concrete, an impregnable fortress.

A place in the person's heart is made for bitterness. To let loose of this would mean entrance into a heavily guarded part of one's personality. The person says, "It belongs there."

I have known precious human beings who held on to bitterness. Perhaps you and I even have a place or two in our hearts especially reserved for a bitter pill we had to swallow.

We have all experienced hurts and injustices (real or imagined). Look closely. Is there some bitterness stowed away in a dungeon of your soul? Perhaps it is taking its toll even now.

When we look at others with compassion, it's surprising how, sooner or later, they begin to resemble us. To sincerely and genuinely help another is to help yourself. The counselor and counselee are the same.

Probably the most unrealistic thing we attempt in life is to be a fixer of other people. Yet there is a ray of sunshine in all of this. I mean, of course, being willing to be fixed ourselves!

Yes, we all have those fortresses inside of us. For some, they are virtually all-consuming. For the rest of us, they amount to being honest enough to admit we need to let go of bitterness.

A great ministry for both the ordained and unordained is to absorb the bitterness of others. Those harboring bitterness are helped by those willing to care and be vulnerable. The bonus is that we, too, find healing.

24   Never Too Much Love

"I love you," the young man said as he put the ring on her finger. He meant it, and she cherished the moment. They were two lovebirds off and running to a golden wedding anniversary.

To the hundreds of couples who have come to me to get married, I always make sure to ask one question in particular: Can I count on you to celebrate your golden wedding anniversary?

It has a sobering effect! Sometimes, like a lightning bolt, it hits them. Can they really lovingly stay together for fifty years?

I have found weddings to be blessed events. The various expressions of love are often inspiring. Yet love takes on a new meaning in the context of five decades.

When I learn that a couple whom I have married is breaking up, it hurts deeply. In fact, sometimes it makes me downright angry. What about "'til death do us part"?

Some believe it is possible to have a deep love for one another, yet still be incompatible. I don't buy that. Perhaps I am just unrealistically romantic. I believe that love between husbands and wives must be overshadowed by God's love, because human love has its limitations. Couples must learn that, I hope, sooner than later.

So today, how is it with you who have been married for quite some time? Are the expressions of love between you—spoken and unspoken—still vital and meaningful? Maybe it's time for a refresher course.

The longevity of a marriage really does depend on whether or not husbands and wives love one another. A loveless marriage depresses everyone. So when you look into your spouse's eyes, say, "I love you."

So what happens when there was once love but there is no longer? Several couples in the process of divorce have told me they have simply fallen out of love. It didn't have to be that way.

A man once summed it up this way: "If I had only looked into my wife's eyes and said, 'I love you,' we would never have divorced." The sad part is that he was probably right.

25   Forgive and Forget

"I will never forgive that bum," she said. The woman was hardened and frustrated by years of living with an alcoholic husband. The love she once felt had long since drifted away.

She felt she was trapped by being too old to get a good-paying job. At least by staying with her husband, she could share a modest home, social security, and pension. She resented him in that she seemed to have no escape.

In a way, she is a prototype of much pain and even rage. The very thing that would make her life better, she refuses to give.

As I have traveled life's hazardous roads with thousands of precious human beings, one thing stands out: to withhold forgiveness is not a helpful answer. Do you agree?

Mind you, I would never condone the abominable actions of an alcoholic spouse. (Help is available for virtually everything today.) But how can you help someone who refuses to forgive?

It's a question that has a haunting ring to it. It may very well be our biggest challenge. As we consult justice and fairness, we begin to see the magnitude of it.

If you or I were in a similar situation as this dear lady, we might not do well either. She has obviously been wronged. Lack of forgiveness seems natural enough, perhaps even right.

Yet our spiritual experiences tell us genuine forgiveness provides a powerful and healthy release. In counseling or spiritual direction, watch someone jump with joy when forgiveness is given.

Her husband may still be a very sick man after she forgives him. However, her attitude will change and so will her view of the Almighty. She will have gained God's gift.

So often good people think they have the right not to forgive. It may take them years to realize this is suicidal. They are aborting a gift from God He wants to bestow.

One suggestion is to forgive everyone of everything every night before you go to sleep. Those who practice it tell of a good night's sleep. Gone is the tension of harboring unforgiveness.

We are not talking about an easy solution . . . or are we? If God wants us to be forgiving, surely the way is provided. God would never leave us to our own devices. We would automatically fail.

Well, how about you and me? We all have those places in our hearts eaten raw by unforgiveness. Accept God's gift within you that enables you to forgive and be thankful.

26   Oh Yes, There Is a Devil

"The devil made me do it," was a favorite line on television for many years. It always got a big laugh. Actually, it became a favorite line in regular conversation.

What continually surprises me is the truth embedded is treated as comedy. My understanding is that there is, in fact, such an evil person deeply involved in all sin.

Maybe you don't see things that way. I have known many people who consider evil and the devil a colossal joke. They don't believe they exist.

Highly educated persons have made a case for the devil simply being a figment of the imagination. Their influence in recent generations has been considerable.

A creature with a pitchfork and horns is a favorite tool for humor. Well, yes, these folks can seem comic, but aren't we only trying to bypass truth? What is it we are trying to avoid?

The Judeo-Christian tradition tells us in no uncertain terms there really is an evil being. The names and labels may differ, but the reality is unavoidable.

Conversely, some go so far as to insist the only problem is negative thinking. The point being all we have to do is consistently think positively and evil evaporates. Sorry, I don't buy that.

I sometimes believe many want to remake basic revelation to Christians into something much more conducive to our natural inclinations. If there is no evil, then temptation is not relevant.

When we give up fundamental understandings given to us over the centuries, we get into trouble. Some seem to go so far as to say, "Man created God." (At least, that is the essence of their thought.)

Strike all the names for the evil force in the Scriptures and what do you find? For me, all that is accomplished is moving the language around. We still have hate and hurt in abundance.

I really like comedy and humor. But I wonder seriously, just maybe the devil did make us do it. So to pause and look at something in depth reveals something significant.

To believe that there isn't a powerful force that seeks only our demise is to ask for trouble. Most of all, we deny the truth of Scripture and even say Jesus didn't know what He was talking about when he spoke of the devil.

27 Trust: An Essential Ingredient

"Trust me" is a common way of saying to someone that we tell the truth. Trust, however, is a slippery commodity in today's world. I tend to be trusting yet realistic, wanting to believe the best about someone.

It goes without saying that trust is absolutely necessary in healthy relationships. For example, a stable family life depends on trust between a husband and wife.

In a larger sense, nations also are subject to this virtue. Imagine Americans living out their lives in a society where trust had become a relic from bygone days. No, trust is important. What if you couldn't trust other people to stop at red lights, or firefighters to fight fires?

Trust is imperative in living a reasonably happy and contented life, and in keeping society intact.

The absence of trust can cause you, me, and others great pain and frustration.

The time to teach and learn about trust is during childhood. A little boy or girl needs to know reliability is present in both parents. When it isn't, God help them!

Conversely, perhaps you have known people like I have, that you virtually trust with your life. They are so mature you just know they are going to be faithful. The circumstances and inconveniences don't matter.

Unhappiness, to a large extent, comes from having no one to trust. If a person lets you down, it can be difficult to trust others.

Those who profess to follow Christ bear a special responsibility to be trustworthy.

28   Excess Can Pulverize Us

"I am going to have that. I am going to possess it at any cost!" the young man said. I admit there have been several times in my life that very sentiment was all too real.

If it is a worthy goal that will benefit others, we're likely on to something good. If it is the kind of possessing that calls ethics into question, however, we'd better re-evaluate our motives.

Greed could be the real issue at hand. Sometimes we don't care who gets hurt; we are going to have what we want! Ambition is a powerful force that, when wielded without boundaries, can have devastating repercussions.

We have to be careful and think through the consequences of our actions. Maybe you are considering a course of action that will impact others. You may be on the verge of moving greedily to possess something you have wanted for a long time. Ask yourself, *Is it worth it?*

Someone has said, "If we are too careful about our actions, we never do anything." That's true, and yet it isn't. Simply "to be" is to have actions, and that's life!

Once in a while we really get involved in heavy rationalizations, don't we? Pure and unadulterated greed has a habit of justifying itself. And money may not be the issue at all. It may be someone else's wife or someone else's husband!

Sometimes a significant goal seems within our grasp. We grab for it and it eludes us. What went wrong and whose fault is it we have failed?

Those of us who have lived some years know to fail may be to succeed. Rudyard Kipling helps us here: " . . . meet with Triumph and Disaster /And treat those two imposters just the same" (*If*).

29   Gaining Balance in Prayer

"It's so hard for me to keep quiet," the lady said to her social group. She knew deep down her incessant talking wasn't helpful.

I suspect many of us can relate. Perhaps it's a nervous habit that we have without even recognizing it. Every now and then, however, it may register that our mouths have been going too long.

Our prayer lives can also be like that. We may tend to keep right on talking to God, as though everything depended on our getting enough words said. It often pays to back off.

In the first place, what are you going to tell God that He doesn't already know? Is it our duty to brief the Lord God of the universe? Sometimes it's as though we think we are a news network. But it's unnecessary. I am convinced He knows all about us before we even open our mouths.

The next time you pray, let God have a word or two. (Of course, He will have the last word anyway!) Silent moments are vital in prayer. They have a way of clearing our agendas and allowing God's agenda to emerge. I always felt the Quakers (Society of Friends) were on to something in their long periods of silence. The Spirit of the living God is given a chance to be heard.

I believe God seldom speaks in actual words. It is His awesome presence that carries the day. The positive presence of God in our prayer lives is of paramount importance.

So, should we never open our mouths in audible prayer? Of course not. Like all of life, our focus on silence is a matter of balance. Ask the dear Lord to guide your every step in prayer. Then spoken words and silence will be in just the right amounts.

30 Keep on Singing

"O, for a thousand tongues to sing," the old gentleman sang with gusto. He loved the song so much he seemed to laugh and cry at the same time. Others relished watching him. Every time he sang it he glowed with the ecstasy of someone taken into another world. It was almost a religious service within itself, entering into worship through his song.

This great hymn was written by Charles Wesley. His brother John was a preacher and the organizer of Methodism. Charles was the hymn writer.

Music in worship should not be underestimated. Great evangelistic preaching in our nation has almost always been linked to inspirational music. There is nothing quite like music to motivate us in worship. Yes, sometimes the angels sing!

In more recent times Dwight L. Moody preached with hymns by Ira Sankey; Billy Graham preached with hymns by George Beverly Shea. It's difficult to imagine each of them without the other. Talk about spiritual electricity!

Perhaps the greatest hymn writers of our time are Bill and Gloria Gaither from Alexandria, Indiana. How could evangelistic meetings be done without their music?

"Jesus, Jesus, Jesus! There's just something about that name!" is sung across our nation. Witness the tears of joy that flow. Note the abandonment to the spiritual world.

"Because He lives, I can face tomorrow" always makes me teary-eyed. It is a way of propelling one into a land we know will always exist for us. Hope abounds.

"Something beautiful, something good" moves us beyond the mundane, sometimes sordid, reality of our times. We know we don't have to be content with sin's presence. Beauty and goodness are by God's design.

Then Bill Gaither wrote the one that melts the hardest of sinners. "He touched me, O He touched me, and O the joy that fills my soul" thrills us again and again. We are made whole.

Yes, there is nothing quite like music to penetrate our thickest armor. God knew this when He breathed the Psalms. The ancient church even used them as their prayer book.

So let's sing more, both inside and outside of our churches. It is a precious way for us to come to terms with our spiritual depths.

"**I**t's time to go," he said. The father and husband was indicating something very important. He was giving the sign to leave one place and go to another.

It seems as though in every family, someone knows when it's time to go. I can remember one of my grandfathers giving the sign at family gatherings. We all seemed to wait on him.

In reflection, it was a kind of rite of passage in a small way that added up to big influence. If he were present, it was his right, even duty, to say those words. That's powerful stuff!

Who in your life gives this signal? In most of our lives, I dare say, the answer is subtle. Yet, we know there is a reality that impacts us day after day. Someone or something tells us that it's time to go.

Should we leave our job or should we keep it? Should we change homes or stay where we are? Should we leave old ways of thinking or move on to other avenues of thought?

I have known persons who sensed death—the ultimate time to go. Maybe the person to leave was a friend or relative of theirs. At any rate, they sensed the death angel had said a transition was coming.

Whether it's a really big matter or those of seemingly little consequence, we all sense transition. The key question, however, is this: Is it you deciding or someone else?

Here's an illustration from my own life. The pastor-parishioner relationship can be among the most powerful of all experiences. This is especially true if the pastor has been there many years. Long pastorates can have joys and problems.

Saying good-bye always has a way of influencing people positively or negatively. I can remember leaving a parish with precious people wanting to know why. I knew it was time to go.

What do you say to a couple who remind you that you confirmed them, married them, and baptized their children? "Who said it was time to go? We cannot get along without you!" they intimated.

Fortunately, the grace of God is always at work in our lives (unless we insist on thwarting it), and He leads our coming and going. This means it is of utmost importance to know when He is transitioning us; listen to when He tells you it's His decision to go. God always knows best.

32   Moderation Isn't Always the Best Policy

"**D**o everything in moderation" is a bit of wisdom shared by most everyone I have ever known. It has found a place in our culture, yes, even in our hearts and minds. But is it reliable?

Is it okay to steal, as long as I don't do it too often? Maybe, if I only steal something once or twice each year, I am a good upstanding citizen. This sounds a little ridiculous.

Is it acceptable to gossip about my neighbor only on Tuesday of each week? Maybe you are thinking, "Oh, get serious!" The truth of the matter is, I am serious.

Is it good behavior to cheat occasionally? Maybe if I only cheat once in a while on a test, that's just expected. Suppose in the future there is no one sitting next to you with the answer?

There is a deeply entrenched attitude today that is always looking for an infraction. What makes the news? Someone may live most of his (her) life in moderation, but it's the exceptions in our lives that are often the most remembered.

Does the current tabloid mentality care about the hundred good deeds or the one misdeed? We both know the answer. To be "temperate" or "moderate" is fraught with uncertainties.

Is moderation the same for you as it is for me? Maybe yes and maybe no.

I remember as a little boy watching real men smoke cigarettes, pipes, and cigars. I remember getting some mixed signals. So I concluded a guy should smoke moderately.

At the same time my dad smoked two packs every day. That seemed more than enough. It made sense to me to smoke just a few cigarettes each day, maybe eight or ten.

So, at the ripe old age of twelve I decided to get started. An older fellow (thirteen) and I divided up a pack of Lucky Strikes. Boy did we smoke up a storm!

Talk about being sick! I pleaded for mercy! Out with this business of moderation and on to avoiding all that nausea and dizziness, making me a total abstainer for fifty years. Some things shouldn't be done . . . even in moderation!

33   Crosses Are Made for Growth

"Oh, stop being a crybaby," one little boy said to another, who had just taken a pretty good beating and was licking his wounds. Mostly self-esteem was at stake.

It doesn't matter if you are eight or eighty, affliction of some kind is always present. To be in this world is to know affliction. We must never settle for this fact and become so negative that it pushes us into needless surrender.

To be put down by forces we cannot control can kill the human spirit. Yet it can sometimes act as a stimulus to begin living a better—much better—life. Affliction can be a spur to victory.

The few truly great people I have known have taken the affliction life dished out and done something constructive with it. They chose not to remain crybabies!

Greatness is especially found in those who have been treated unfairly, even maliciously, by forces beyond their control. They simply refuse to be defeated, and the heavens smile in accord.

From a Christian viewpoint this has something to do with carrying our own crosses. It is a daily, sacred undertaking.

Embrace your cross and treat it as an opportunity for growth. Have you ever thought what Christ's resurrection would be like without His crucifixion? I dare say it might very well be an empty victory. It would be nice, but lacking in real power.

Of course, what is an affliction for one is not for another. That's for you and God to sort out. It is in the privacy of your own inner sanctuary that you discover the truth.

Will tomorrow be better for you? Do you want tomorrow to be better for you? I hope so, because a better tomorrow for you means one for me and many others.

Souls that have no cross to carry come before God lacking substance. Be optimistic in whatever circumstances you find yourself. Nothing is ever too big for God to handle. But be patient, fighting your battles with a love that will not let you go.

Communication Is Essential

"I'm sure that's what he said," I heard from the booth next to mine in the restaurant. This comment started me thinking about the importance of communication.

Communication is a two-way street. Does the listener always hear what the speaker says? Try to count the times that what you thought was said really wasn't.

Was each major word carefully defined before a statement was made? Was everyone listening in complete concentration? We all know the answers, don't we?

Let's take a common word like "dog." Is the dog a schnauzer, poodle, collie, dachshund, terrier, or bulldog? By now we begin to get the picture.

The same principle applies to correctly interpreting body language. "I know he rejected me because he turned his back on me." That could be an erroneous assumption. Do you suppose his back was hurting and he needed to sit differently?

"Her face was red and she was so angry at her mother." Do you suppose she was having an allergic reaction?

"There sat the old duffer whispering funny things to that young woman. The dummy thought he was a real ladies' man!" Do you suppose she was his daughter? Or that he actually could have been amusing?

"That policeman really has it in for me. Every time I drive around town, there he is in my rearview mirror." Perhaps he saw someone tailing you and he is providing protection?

Sometimes we are just wrong about communication. Yes, sometimes we even decide beforehand what we are going to assume by things we see or hear. It is sometimes difficult to give the benefit of the doubt. We need to be patient with one another. What seems to be communicated may be completely misinterpreted.

Celebrate the good that people intend to communicate, and always seek to provide good on your part. Communication gets a lot better when we remember that first or second impressions can be way off base. And use that two-way street of communication to inquire of someone what he or she really meant.

35 Instant Gratification Is a Problem

"He eats like a pig." Gluttony is such a nasty word, isn't it? Who would want to be called a glutton?

Gluttony is among the seven deadly sins. But who among us is willing to consider overeating in that way? In our culture, a myriad of foods and drinks are almost instantaneously available. Feeling uptight? Grab a chocolate bar. Feeling pressed for time? We can grab hamburgers, french fries, and soft drinks at a drive-through window.

How do we celebrate? We can go out and buy a really big meal. Now, don't we feel better having gulped down all that tasty and satisfying stuff?

So often we go about our lives without realizing this connection between overeating and the day in which we live. Our need to feel better is brought into play. Our need to lessen the pain of living is present. We try to achieve peace through instant gratification.

The next time you've "gotta" have another big piece of fried chicken or dish of rich pudding, simply wait. We need to slow down today's powerful tendency towards instant gratification. This can be done by simply putting a pressing desire on hold. This allows us time to realize what is happening so we can make a conscious decision of whether to use food in a gluttonous manner or to deal with what's really driving our actions. If we are willing to be driven on, we know what is happening. Personal decisions are right, necessary, and God-given.

36   Worry Is a Robber

"**Y**ou worry too much," a fellow said to me the other day. Of course, I like to think of it as *concern* for people that makes me have sleepless nights. Maybe it's a bit of both. Are you able to tell the difference in your own life? It isn't always easy to tell the difference.

There is a difference between worry and natural concerns. Worry is a negative exercise that leads us no place, except to a nervous breakdown.

Concern is necessary. It is true that we are to be rightfully concerned about some situations and people. For instance, parents should have a healthy concern for their sons and daughters.

The downside of worry is seen in a number of ways. Its pervasive presence keeps reminding us there are better ways (much better) for people to spend time and energy. Worry robs us of valuable time when we could be doing something far more constructive.

What about all the misdirected energy? When you are exhausted and have nothing to show for it, it is worry that is the culprit and not concern.

Worry can become a habit. I believe we sometimes deceive ourselves by feeling good about worrying. Silly? Well, no. Some people assume that worry shows compassion and concern, and that it is protection. If one worries enough, one will uncover all the negative possibilities and then know how to deal with them. That's just not true. Yet there are people who in the school of life have always majored in worry. They can even feel martyr-like.

Some people even worry about their prayer lives. *Did I pray long enough and did I say the right words? Since I have so many faults, maybe God doesn't hear my prayers at all.*

I am a firm believer that God calls us to be concerned; He never calls us to be worried about anything or anyone. Saint Peter says, "Don't be afraid of anyone and don't worry."

37 Turn Gossip into Good

"Have you heard . . ." is a common way of launching into gossip. There seems to be a deep-seated need in many people to talk about others. Sometimes we're even caught in it before we know it!

Gossip can ruin. It can destroy entire careers and families. Its potential for evil is almost like the presence of the devil, laughing and gloating with glee.

Perhaps we should seek to do something positive about gossip. When we hear someone tear into someone else, why not turn that into a positive event? We can creatively manage the hurtful and destructive tendency to gossip. Redirect it and bring it under control.

We shouldn't hold still for it when bad things are stated or even implied about people. This doesn't mean that we should raise our voices. All we need to do is put on our thinking caps.

We should always strive to move slanderous remarks away from evil intent. Sometimes humor is effective. At other times mildly disagreeing with the critic does the job. Compliment the person being attacked or lay out options of why a person is the way he or she is. Talk about the foibles of life and our need to be compassionate and not judge.

The next time gossip is gaining a foothold, offer a simple, silent prayer and then jump into the conversation. God knows the situation can be changed.

I have hopes for gossip, rightly directed. We can practice making it into a tool for maturity. It can be tamed and it can be useful among those of us who believe God can change anything.

38   Take Another Look at Your Work

"I just love my work," the nurse said confidently and with a healthy pride. I'll bet she didn't mean she loved it in a romantic way or because it consumed her body and soul. More likely, she meant opportunity, talent, and energy came together. Things fell into place.

Work is important to human beings. Those of us in the helping professions often work around the clock. Frequently, we don't maintain a clear-cut line between work activity and other activities or thoughts. We seem to be in the harness all the time.

There is a danger of mental or physical breakdown due to uninterrupted work. How did this come about and where does all of this take us in a world that appears to speed up every day?

If you are past fifty and reflect upon the hard work done by our parents and grandparents, you may scratch your head in disbelief. I certainly do. How, in the name of high heaven, did they work so hard and for such long hours?

I continue to have great admiration, especially for those who worked on the farms and in factories. Who has recently plowed with horses and milked by hand? Remember the tough days on the assembly lines?

Despite the hard physical work earlier generations experienced, they didn't seem to have the mental health issues our society has today. Yet perhaps no one wants to return to the "good ole days." They were not always that good. Many things were unpredictable, and built-in protections hardly existed. Much has changed.

Let's be honest though. There is a certain nostalgia about all of this. We wonder if we have lost something important. I, for one, believe we have suffered loss, yet I have trouble expressing it.

In a way, I suspect this something has to do with our souls, individually and collectively. It isn't that we have become a nation of loafers. It isn't that each of us feels he or she doesn't work hard enough.

I believe it has to do with meaning and integration. No one's job is unimportant. Every job we have should be connected to our personhood and aid us in becoming whole persons.

Despite our best efforts, unfortunately many today work at jobs at home and away that appear to mean little and add little to our wholeness (or should we say holiness?). You and I must do better.

39   Don't Give Up on Promises

"**W**hen you grow up, do what you promise to do," his mother always told him. That stuck with him and now he was an old man. He had often thanked his mother for that.

How good are we at keeping our promises today? Do memories conveniently fail us from time to time? Sometimes I think memories have grown awfully short.

One reason we slip out of promises today is the sheer movement of the population.

A daughter promises to visit her invalid father every week. But she moves and is now more than a thousand miles away. The promise simply has to be broken.

Some of us can remember when many — perhaps a majority of us — lived in a rather well-defined area. That area kept us close to one another. A two-hour drive covered it.

Not so today, and promises often have to be amended and even broken. We don't intend to do harm to our integrity. Nevertheless, we have to learn to make peace with reality.

A second reason we sometimes fail in keeping our promises is the force of human interaction. It seems we are saying so much so often, we can forget a promise. It becomes unimportant.

I am sympathetic with those who hurry about to make a living and forget a promise once made. We get filled with schedules and information. Sometimes, there isn't room for anything else. I really do not believe in many cases that this is intentional. It is a fact of our existence.

But promises are important, even today. Don't we run nearly every volunteer and not-for-profit organization on promises? Is our employment a promise to work hard and professionally for our employer? Try to live in today's world without promises.

It's critical we keep promises to ourselves and others. When we do, the same result is realized as it was by our grandparents: respect for ourselves and others is enhanced.

What promise will you make today that will benefit all concerned? Will you stand by it until hell freezes over? I hope so, because our children and grandchildren need to witness that. God never breaks a promise and He hopes we won't either.

"**I** am having a panic attack!" the young woman blurted out. While she could have been using exaggeration, panic attacks are real and seem to impact more people today than years ago.

The anxiety level is often very high for otherwise very productive people. To be on our last nerve or at the end of our rope is common today.

Compassion and a listening ear go a long way in helping those afflicted by a high level of anxiety. Compassion has to be communicated, and listening to others has to be cultivated. Anxiety is lessened by genuineness.

Do you suppose there are panic attacks among the Amish? Their simple and wholesome lifestyle appears much different from the way most of us live. I love their striving for purity.

Perhaps we would all be better off imitating, at least to some extent, the way they live. I, for one, certainly have a tremendous admiration for them. Biblical truth comes alive in a special way.

Of course, I am not suggesting we all abandon our cars and travel in buggies pulled by horses. I am suggesting the Amish have a thing or two to teach us.

Before you go out and spend a bundle of money to cure your latest panic attack, ponder a more simple lifestyle. Some answers may be as close as the nose on your face.

"Have no anxiety about anything, but in everything by prayer and supplication with thanksgiving let your requests be made known to God" (Phil. 4:6 RSV).

Living and Dying Victoriously

"**N**othing is certain but death and taxes," we've often heard people quote. One is a persistent reality and reminder; the other is an ongoing irritant.

You will die and I will die. That may sound trite and just another mouthing of the obvious. Believe me it isn't, and dying deserves top priority and now.

I say this not as a scare tactic, but as a means for us simply to accept a basic fact. There is no need to be morbid, nor to dwell upon the event all the time.

However, I suppose there is nothing so intimate as the time in history you and I go to meet our Creator.

Ever think about dying? Any idea who will attend your funeral? Who would you like to be there? What will people say about your life and the way you lived it?

These are inquiries we don't necessarily like to pose, but in a way, they are often with us. Even the most hard-nosed know death, in time, will come. There is no avoiding or evading.

One's passing really should be a celebration. It should be a time for others to reflect upon your good deeds. It should also be a time for loved ones to shed tears of loss.

As we grow older, we wonder about the moment of death. Will there be pain and a sense of helplessness? Where will I be when this happens and who will observe?

Truly, death is the great leveler for all of us. The rich and the poor, the wise and the unwise, the religious and irreligious are claimed by the death angel. We all become equal.

The great Saint Paul had a way of putting all of this into proper focus for the Christian. He says, "Whether I live or die I belong to Christ" (Rom. 14:8, author paraphrase).

I can't speak for you, dear friends, but it really seems to me the apostle has it right. To be a faithful follower of the Christ is a win-win situation. We are always winners.

What songs do you want sung at your funeral? I think songs are very important and need your advance planning. As for me, please sing the "Battle Hymn of the Republic" at the top of your voices.

42 Celebrate All Seasons

"**S**pring is just around the corner," she said with a big smile on her face. She loved spring and all the newness that came forth. The whole world seemed to be a better place.

Every year it was the same. Summers were entirely too hot; winters were too cold; and fall reminded her of dying. Ah, but, spring was the most blessed time of the year.

The flowers bloomed; the birds sang more; the grass became green; and the smell of newly plowed ground was like expensive perfume.

Then one day she ran across some powerful words in the book of Ecclesiastes: "Everything that happens in this world happens at the time God chooses" (Eccles. 3:1 GNT). Light bulb!

A sobering thought hit her like a ton of bricks. Had she been living her life based on three months out of the year? It didn't seem right to tolerate nine months just to enjoy three. To live for three months out of the year was like living only 25 percent of the time. It dawned on her that just maybe all twelve months were necessary and pretty terrific. If there were twelve months of spring, when would there be a harvest?

She decided to make the most of all of the months. Spring was still great and wonderful. Yet, so was summer with its heat; fall with its marvelous colors; and winter with its stark magnificence.

Now, think carefully, dear friends. This realization applies to more than just the seasons.

If accepted properly and positively, what in this whole wide world can we discount? God provides potential blessings beyond counting. We are not in a position to question His providence.

Should we make fun of our hamburgers because we can't afford steak? You have fifteen sparrows in your trees and no robins. Does that mean we watch endlessly for a robin that may not show?

We are given so very much. Yet sometimes we get picky and put down that which is intended for our enhancement. How much better it is to celebrate the seasons and all God's gifts!

43   A Promise to Keep

"Until death do us part" kept running through the man's mind. That was about the only part of their wedding he remembered—that, and how nervous he had felt.

They had now been married almost seven years. For some reason he had an unsettling feeling that wouldn't go away.

Why did he feel so uneasy? He couldn't explain it, but the brief words from the wedding service kept his mind in a state of agitation. He looked at his five-year-old son and two-year-old daughter. They looked like both him and his wife. Life really had gone smoothly.

Soon, his wife arrived home from work in a cheery mood. Then something happened.

She slumped down on the floor, unconscious. He called 911. At the hospital, he was told that his twenty-eight-year-old wife had suffered a stroke. She couldn't say a word that was understandable, nor could she move her legs. There had been no warning signs, and her husband was totally stunned.

As time passed, it was obvious his wife would never be the same again. Her body, even after months of therapy, would not respond enough to make much difference.

Their lives radically changed. The phrase "until death do us part" once again entered his mind. Would he be willing to stay close by her side? He wondered about his patience and the many limitations.

He had never felt quite so confused in all of his young life.

Do I want to do this? Is this really required of me? Maybe the wedding vow is really just a nice thing to say but it wasn't at all intended to be literal. Surely a nice, healthy young man such as myself doesn't deserve this.

He had just about decided to get out of their marriage, when it occurred to him that his promise was made before God and to his bride. His new cross to stay married then became bearable.

44   Some Things You Don't Need to Know

"Go on about your business," a lady, clearly annoyed, said to her part-time friend. This was one of those cases where the dividing line between curiosity and real concern was thin.

Human relations always fascinate me. The good Lord made us so different and yet so much alike. One of the most delicate problems, I've observed, is the difference between crass curiousness and caring concern. Patience is often required to tell them apart.

In church life, I know no other issue as detrimental to human relationships. The need to know on the part of some is phenomenal—even when it's none of their business.

Interactions can become explosive because one person persists in knowing areas of someone else's life. Explosions erupt. Love seems to turn to hate and friendship is dissolved.

The hurt that emanates when a person deliberately enters uninvited into another's personal life is hard to describe, and the truth is hard to come by.

Frankly, it is more than a shame. It is a tragedy, and largely because a person simply cannot control the need to know something about another human being. So how do you deal with the situation? Only God's mercy helps.

Those who are not hurt may smile and not see the harm . . . until it happens to them. Then a whole new world opens!

And what is your part in putting a quietus to such things? It's poor grammar, but the fact is it "ain't" easy. (To be blunt, it can be downright difficult.)

The Letter of James is a big help in terms of understanding the wrong use of human speech and confidences. When you combine the wisdom of James with the following questions, healing can come.

In a conversation involving personal and private matters, be quick to ask yourself two questions: *Why do I want to know about this? Is it for the right reasons?*

Now, memorize both questions and write them on your heart. Apply this discipline at all times and every place. If you are faithful in this, you'll experience more peace, the people you speak with will experience more peace, and a revolution will take place in every life you touch.

Be Careful About Your Agenda

"It's easier to get forgiveness than it is permission," the ambitious young man said. His superiors looked the other way when he developed some questionable projects, because he was always successful.

He had figured out how to circumvent authority figures and power centers in order to meet his objectives. He was very proud of this skill, always trying to plan bigger and better future exploits. He eventually despised anyone in his way, especially those representing institutions.

Others applauded his success. He was beating the system and that was important to them. He was something of a celebrity to other ambitious people. He had quite a following after several years.

Although he understood God was good, the man was also convinced God favored him in all circumstances. In his mind, God had become a doting grandfather who handed him lollipops and thought His grandson could do no wrong.

Then the inevitable happened. Those in high places grew tired of looking like fools. Doubt then entered the minds of those who tried to imitate his method of success. With a loud thud, he failed.

As he was licking his wounds and crying his heart out, the man came upon this passage in Psalms: "If the Lord does not build the house, the work of the builders is useless . . ." (Ps. 127:1 GNT). He had been on the wrong road all the time!

It had taken years, but in the twinkling of an eye he finally understood. He couldn't change the past, but he could seek God's guidance for the future.

"**B**eauty is only skin deep," we've all heard. Genuine beauty is found in the depths of a person.

That being said, why does our culture spend billions of dollars on appearance? It seems we've become a nation obsessed with looks rather than substance. Maybe we should recommend that everyone just be plain, clean, and neat for one week as an experiment. That might disrupt the entire economy!

I often wonder if our attempts to look just right mask serious unhappiness or an impoverished soul.

Since so many people tend to whirl and swirl through life, we could easily become people merely concerned with surface matters. It's tragic that so many become obsessed with people simply by their appearance, although they seem to have no substance. Go look at the celebrities pictured on magazine covers if you doubt this.

But what I'm concerned about is what happens to us if we start to model our lives on people without substance and don't consider deeper matters. Often the only corrective is solitude. We simply have to take time to be alone and focus on what ultimately counts. Isn't this life preparation for the next?

Frankly, I admire people who dress well and take excellent care of their skin and hair. To a degree, it is important how we look to one another and to ourselves. I wonder how we look to God.

Praying for Salvation

"**P**lease, more time," she pleaded. Her body was tiring and her knees hurt. She had been praying for so long that she had forgotten the passage of time.

Death was coming to a dear friend and she was concerned. Her friend had not practiced the Christian faith in anyone's memory.

Their friendship went back many years, all the way to high school. Now they both were beyond seventy.

The woman prayed her heart out that her friend would not leave this world unprepared. She implored God to give her friend more time to repent.

The hardest thing about this crisis was that her friend had lived morally, a life virtually above reproach. However, except for weddings, funerals, and Mother's Day, she never attended church.

The woman continued to pray for her longtime friend as the hours became days. God was earnestly asked to provide more time. Wouldn't it be a terrible thing for her to be lost and have to spend eternity without God? This should not happen!

Some of us have faced similar situations. The people in question were known by all to be loving, kind, and charitable. But only God knew the condition of their eternal souls.

As a pastor for well over four decades, I learned not to send people to heaven or hell in what I thought. I also learned we must be faithful to the Scriptures and seek to be genuinely helpful enablers. This means don't judge but be ever diligent as you present the Gospel. This is God's business and far out of our jurisdiction.

Being saved can be many things to many people. The real question seems always the same: Have you come to terms with the Father through Jesus Christ, our Savior and Lord?

Maybe you have a friend who needs more time to enter the bliss of salvation. Maybe in your understanding it is a full blown crisis. Do what God calls you to do, no more and no less.

48   A Matter of Perspective

"**H**e had a hard life," his granddaughter pointed out, regret and pain in her voice.

He worked twelve hours a day, six days a week. There was one week for vacation from work. He spent time with his family but they never traveled far.

It was late-nineteenth and early-twentieth centuries. World War I was on the horizon. Grandfather worked those seventy-two-hour weeks under very harsh conditions. In his day, labor unions had little imprint. There was one boss and he called the shots. To be sick a day was to get a cut in pay.

Factory life was not only dirty, it was dangerous. That didn't seem to matter much. If a man wanted to make a living for his family, he had to put up with more than some can even imagine. Her grandfather had eight mouths to feed—himself, his wife, and their six children.

She delved into family history, uncovering records and notes left by her grandmother. The more she studied about his day and time, the more she was impressed. Her grandfather seemed to have been a wonderful man but she felt sorry for him.

Her grandmother wrote about taking the children to Sunday school, dressed in their best clothes. Her notes told how proud he was of them every Sunday morning. He seldom went along but watched carefully as they walked down a gravel road, rain or shine, for a couple of miles.

When she ran across some of her grandfather's own scribbles, she struck pure gold. Every word he had written—some misspelled—gave thanks for a good life.

With tears of joy, the woman's perspective changed to match that of her dear grandfather. She had learned a valuable lesson in gratitude.

49   Basketball All Pervasive
When You Persevere

"Call it a day," his mother shouted at him. He was playing basketball by himself, repeatedly shooting the ball through the hoop on the side of the barn.

It was also getting dark and the farm boy could hardly see to shoot. Instinct helped a lot but really not enough. His mother said his supper was getting cold.

If you grew up in central Indiana quite some years ago, this situation was normal. Playing basketball, especially in the little schools, was like a religion. Shooting hoops was part of the air breathed and the soil tilled.

And if you were on a team, well, to have to sit on the bench for very long was an absolute humiliation. The unquestioned state of affairs was that you practiced long and hard in the gym or at home.

Not to make the varsity by the junior year was almost unforgivable in the little schools. To make it and then have to be sent down to the second team was pure hell.

Some guys, regardless of size, were tough as pine knots. Believe it or not, playing basketball could be better than eating! To call it quits, supper or no supper, was not an alternative.

As some of us assess those days, we recall a few really outstanding players and games. The memory, however, is of the experience itself.

Long hours in poorly heated and lighted gymnasiums were more the rule than the exception. We farm boys walked to and from gyms, sometimes for miles in those days, always alert to some farmer's dog which didn't take kindly to us. Everyone I know would label them maturing times, from which we benefited.

To be sure, in this life we all need to know when to call it a day, but please be sure the day is over. Many miss a lot by not persevering, not walking the second and third mile.

50 Don't Be Naive

"**T**errorism doesn't scare me in the least," he stated with unwavering confidence. He had just graduated from college, and like many of us at one time, was off to make his fortune.

This terrorist thing was all a matter of staying prepared and not letting down our guard. He saw the United States as somewhat vulnerable, but nothing he should lose any sleep over.

Hadn't we always victoriously emerged from wars — big, little, and otherwise — and gone our way to peacetime? Manpower (and womanpower) and superior weapons were the keys, he opined.

September 11 was over and done with. Future problems had been assessed; there was nothing to get excited about. Everything was under control and progress was in the air.

His youthful optimism was admirable. The trouble was, he didn't realize that almost anyone in the United States can be killed at most any time.

In his self-focused quest for success, he was blindsided by natural ambition and an understanding of history that left much to be desired.

As he rode his bicycle along Lake Michigan, it didn't occur to him that someone could drop him with a powerful rifle from several yards away and never be caught. Of course, a sniper with a rifle wouldn't have to be a terrorist. There are individuals and groups in our country who inexplicably hate and apparently have no connection to terrorist cells. The truth is that terrorism is so widespread we may all be closely affected in time. Unfortunately, that's realistic.

There is literally no place to hide and be absolutely certain attacks and death will not occur. This is made plain by those who sacrifice their lives in a radical fashion. Apparently, some people are ready to die for their causes. In some cases, death is seen as a quicker way to heaven or paradise!

The built-in hate against the United States and others is hard for us to grasp. We are generous people and it's difficult for our culture to understand such hate.

Unfortunately, circumstances now take us where we all prefer not to go—summoned to be prepared as never before.

Heeding God's Warning

"The heat is getting to me," she commented to herself as sweat fell from her face. The eighty-year-old woman was at work in her flower garden filled with a variety of inspirations.

Her neighbors just loved to come by and take a good look. Viewing the gorgeous display was almost a worshipful experience.

The woman had worked hard and was devoted to bringing her gift to the neighborhood. But she was getting too hot. The sun was coming down with full force and the humidity was extremely high.

Overcome by the heat, down she went, collapsing headfirst into her azaleas. A neighbor walked by soon after and discovered her limp body. The woman had suffered a stroke.

In the weeks of convalescence that followed, the dear lady began to admit something to herself. She had overdone it and was paying the price.

She had forewarning. By the end of the previous summer, she could tell that her health had waned. The heat then had negatively affected her. She continued to push herself, though, because she wanted to continue her ministry of flowers.

In retrospect, she knew that God had warned her to slow down, but she had not heeded His advice. The woman regretted her choice. Her life would never be the same.

Many of us have done the same. When doing some really good things for others and loving every minute of it, we frequently succumb to the temptation of not heeding the Lord's prompting.

Even though our intentions are good, we often extend ourselves beyond what the dear Lord expects of us.

Looking for the Good

"**A**lways look for something good," his much older, adoring sister admonished him. She knew from experience that little was accomplished by being critical.

The young fellow in question had entered a phase of teenage years filled with negatives, at least, for him. His sister watched with chagrin and tried to help.

Some days, his attitude was truly unbelievably bad. He couldn't find a good thing to say about anybody, and that included her. But in place of scolding, she spoke kindly. Even humor didn't help much. He was hellbent, so to speak, on proving there was not much good—if any—in every person he knew. Then he would give them—and sometimes complete strangers—heck.

It was like a disease. While others in his age group were likewise bent somewhat in the same direction, he was easily the most negative. Everywhere he looked, he saw only pile after pile of defects.

He was just as hard on himself. He went to class knowing in advance he was going to fail. He played cards with the guys and knew again in advance he was going to lose.

Some people only see negatives. To justify their opinions, they box themselves into a corner and proclaim if they had this or that, they wouldn't be as negative.

Given some time on our knees, we know the truth about that one. It's a serious internal problem, isn't it? When our spiritual lives are at a low ebb, it's tempting to see only the bad. God seems distant and we are not sure our religion makes all that much difference.

Well, let's test the sister's well-known advice. Is there something good in everybody? Well, we are made in God's image, and that is totally good.

Furthermore, God didn't create you and me to flounder in negativity and defeatism. Surely Jesus the Christ was not crucified and then arose from the dead for us to live in gloom and pessimism.

Let us begin changing our thought patterns not by manipulation of emotions or by telling ourselves to get better. Neither one nor the other will work very long. What will work is placing ourselves completely in God's hands and accepting His peace, joy, and hope. Then we will see God in others and they'll see Him in us.

53   The Turn of a Phrase

"You look like the last rose of summer," the old gentleman commented to his wife of sixty years. He meant no disrespect but tried to let her know she didn't look well.

Well, she didn't take kindly to the remark and told him so in no uncertain terms.

As he rocked away in his favorite chair, he tried to think of some way to turn this little encounter into something positive. At last he came up with an idea.

He told his wife that the last rose of summer was a way of looking forward to fall. That's when the inspiring and variegated colors would appear. He was very descriptive about all the beauty that was to come.

She quickly caught on to her husband's attempt at making up for his poor choice of words. Before she knew it, she was feeling better. They both chuckled and decided her looking like the last rose of summer wasn't that bad after all.

Their conversation soon led to discussing a short trip. The maps were out in the blink of an eye, and they planned a long weekend at the lodge. The elderly couple became winners in a little game which might have become a big deal.

Do we all do as well with those little tiffs? When our feathers get ruffled we need to make a conscious effort to be positive. It is natural to be reluctant to turn the other cheek. All we need is a little creativity and humility.

54   Betrayal Is So Costly

"She was my wife!" he cried out hysterically. With glassy eyes, he was so distraught that his coworkers thought surely she had been killed tragically in an accident.

They didn't know his wife. She worked across the city and several miles from his office. There must have been hundreds of thousands of people between them.

He hadn't been employed there all that long, but he was well respected for his work ethic and personal behavior. They wanted to help him but what could they do? He didn't elaborate.

Some expected to learn of her funeral. Others kept trying to find out the very painful problem.

Within a few days, his condition became worse and he became incapable of concentrating on his work. The hysteria subsided but now he only stared out the window, usually disoriented. Apparently, she had not died or they'd have heard.

Into the third day, his boss told him to go on a leave of absence—to do whatever was necessary to get him out of the office. The words hardly registered with him and he prepared to be on his way.

Then, as the man was going out the door, he stopped and looked back at them. In a kind of stupor that masked a pain deep within his soul, he explained. He had accidentally found his wife with his best friend at a motel on the other side of the vast city. The two of them had spent the night together. He promised not to kill himself or them, but he would seek an immediate divorce.

His hurt was so pervasive, his face was contorted. They had been married more than ten years.

He never saw anything amiss. His respect and admiration for her had been at a lofty level all those years. Perhaps, as some would say, he was terribly naïve.

This is an experience of male rage, pain, and disillusionment many women probably do not and cannot relate to. For a good and faithful man, as he was, he may have felt it worse than death.

Infidelity is always painful for a loving husband. It may be the most excruciating suffering he'll ever experience.

55   We All Make False Starts

"Another false start," the fellow in the stands said dejectedly. His favorite football team had just been penalized some more yards. He was angry and disappointed.

Those of us who follow football know the feeling. Our team was all set up to get a better position to score and what happens? The end zone is now further away than ever.

A thinking person sooner or later picks up on the truth of this football fact for everyday living. Many of us seem to go about making too many false starts.

Why do you think people make false starts? There are probably as many answers as there are people. We can note the similarities, but how about the uniqueness of each setback?

Sometimes marriages end up in divorce because they were unsound from the beginning. In a matter of weeks it becomes obvious that two people are not going to make it.

Could this false start have been prevented? Having spent time with hundreds of couples over the years, I believe the answer is *yes* and *no*.

The union of two persons, regardless of sincerity and honesty, does not guarantee a gain in yardage in the game of life. Many factors, mostly intangibles, come to the surface.

Sometimes people seem to suffer false starts in occupation and profession. Years ago, how a person made a living was a permanent issue. Today, it seems failures and disappointments can pile up.

Fortunately—and unfortunately—today's workforce has almost unlimited opportunity. Entire areas of study and labor exist today that I never knew about at Ball State years ago. The good, practical aspect of work opportunities is the almost unbelievable flexibility of being able to change jobs and careers. The not-so-great side is the temptation not to work long enough in a position to know if it is for you.

All of life is a learning experience and there are times we have to stay a while to know more about who and what we are. Our greatest asset to prevent false starts is a solid, ongoing prayer life.

Whether in marriage or vocation, never allow anyone to pronounce a false start upon you. Always question your critics, well-meaning or otherwise.

I have known several folks who made false starts. Through astute behavior, however, they eventually scored touchdowns. Be quick to do your own assessment and never stop learning.

"Keep Christ in Christmas!" she kept insisting. Generally, her message was met with applause and obvious affirmation.

We hear that statement often during the days leading up to Christmas, yet I find it raises an interesting question.

Is anyone really powerful enough to take Christ out of Christmas? Think about it.

I don't know an organization with that much influence.

God the Father revealed His Son in the person of Jesus Christ two thousand years ago. That fact is fixed in history and our belief systems. Nothing can take that away.

While it may be necessary to defend our theological position, real and complete power is in the hands of the living God. He put the Christ in Christmas—without the Babe of Bethlehem, there wouldn't *be* a celebration known as Christmas. We need to be careful we don't give power to those who oppose the priority of Christ.

Yes, and we need to hold steady before those who want His name obliterated!

When I listen to the debate about keeping Christ in Christmas, I have no fear whatsoever. His coming and that celebration shall always be a mainstay.

Are you and I going to be prevented from worshipping the Babe in Bethlehem? In the United States, the separation of church and state, as well as religious freedom, are in place for all to see.

We live in a great nation, which even in its trials and tribulations, continually provides us with the guarantee of expressions of belief. It seems to me that is very noble and worthwhile.

Maybe the concept of keeping Christ in Christmas isn't the problem we should concentrate on. Maybe our society's over-emphasis on Santa Claus is a bigger and more subtle threat. Hmmm . . .

57   Be Careful About Revenge

"Oh, get lost," she said angrily. The guy was a nuisance to her and other women at their place of work.

Her employer knew a little about the situation, but treaded lightly. The fellow was excellent at his work and made plenty of money for the company. Had he been dilatory and nonproductive in his assignment, the decision to get rid of the nuisance would have been simple.

Yet what was he doing that was unacceptable?

One might say he was insulting and even demeaning. Another could say, "boys will be boys." Romeo thought himself merely playful and enlivening a dreary and over-worked group of people. So, where do we go?

Obviously, women should never have to work under such conditions. In this case, his behavior is giving the employer problems, but because of his worth to the company, his absence might cause problems as well.

Eventually, the problem came to a head. He was confronted and his job changed, putting him on the road for days at a time. He apologized to everyone.

That did not pacify the woman. She wanted him punished, preferably fired, with a dark cloud over his next employment. So even though he could no longer rile her, she wanted justice, or some would say, revenge.

The grace of God is never far away. After a time, it dawned on her that she should forgive. She was a well-paid and respected worker. His sub-par behavior had not in any sense hurt her reputation, and in forgiving, she could also move on.

"Over the river and through the woods," the elderly man repeated. His eyes would light up and his countenance would take on an angelic cast. Those around him smiled in approval.

He had been in the nursing home for several months. His children and grandchildren had not abandoned him, but they didn't see him often.

His wife had died some years ago from cancer and her final days were not at all pleasant. While they had had a good marriage of fifty-plus years, he wanted, deep down, to blot out the terrible last days.

So he dug into the wellsprings of his early boyhood days. James Whitcomb Riley's phrase regarding holiday excursions was something he had never forgotten. Now it encouraged him to revel in bygone days.

He remembered vividly the excitement and expectation of going to his grandparents for Thanksgiving, Christmas, and other events. Actually, they had crossed a river and drove through a wood!

The stock market had crashed and the Great Depression was well underway. His parents and grandparents were small town folks or farmers. They were affected by the hard times, but family gatherings went on.

He remembered one of his best gifts at Christmas was a little decorative belt made from walnut shells, carefully shellacked, and strung together with a sturdy string to hold them in place.

Grandfather had made them with his own hands. With or without money, Grandfather was ingenious. And really there was so little money at that time, his dad said he had forgotten what it looked like!

Riley's little series of words carried him into a land long gone and yet still very present in his memory. "Golly, those were good days," he told those about him. He also relished remembering the food they had at those precious gatherings. The menfolk killed rabbits, squirrels, quail, and an occasional pheasant. Those fellows were skilled! Wow, could those ladies come up with delicious dishes! Fried chicken was a standard. He hardly ever recalled anyone going to a grocery. That made sense because no one had much money, but even a penny bought some things.

He recalled hard times, such as when Uncle Bill was gored by a bull, and challenges, like dealing with a team of horses that thought plowing was beneath their dignity. But everyone managed somehow and bickering was off limits.

Once in a while, after romping around in his private world of yesterday, the old gentleman would begin to sing. A bit off key, he would burst into "Precious memories, how they linger . . ."

59   Insistence Might Not Be the Right Way to Go

"I want a piece of the action," the middle-aged entrepreneur insisted. He had been very successful in his business investments. Why wasn't there a place for him in this one?

The new restaurant was going to be a dandy. He especially wanted to be able to go in after it was open and crow a bit about being one of the owners.

His ambition was well-known throughout the community. His need for recognition and acceptance as a successful businessman was also obvious. Most everyone knew him.

Therefore, the investors eventually made a place for him. They had to create a somewhat larger building. The additional space was problematic, but he got a piece of the action.

Early on, people flocked to it and most were complimentary. Then, as rather expected, business began to level off. After a year, it was never full, except on special occasions.

People loved to go there. The food was excellent and the service was well above average. But it became noticeable the building was just too big and space was going to waste.

In another year, those forty seats that rarely had people sitting in them became known as "Charley's folly." Most everyone who had lived there knew he had insisted on a piece of the action. Outsiders even began to ask about the restaurant with "Charley's folly" in it.

He became less seen in public and never went into the restaurant anymore. Sadly, the community seemed to remember Charley for his folly more than anything else.

Just maybe, when we make others find a place for us, things don't go very well. Perhaps to be left out might be the best for all concerned.

60   Foibles of Human Beings

"Say it isn't so," he kept muttering to a few other men around him. He had been deeply hurt by a situation not of his own making. The gloom was heavy.

It is said during the Chicago Black Sox scandal of 1919, little boys would come up to Shoeless Joe Jackson. They would hopefully remark, "Say it isn't so, Joe." Their hero had disappointed them.

Jackson was one of the great baseball players of the time. A poor boy who grew up to become perhaps the best natural hitter the game has ever known was caught helping throw the 1919 World Series. His career was over; we will never know how many records Shoeless Joe Jackson might have set.

As you and I go through the various phases of our lives, we know how those boys felt. Someone is guilty of a deed and we are terribly let down. We desperately want them to say it isn't so.

Church history provides examples galore of those who devastate others by their failures. Young and idealist pastors, glued to a talented superior, can be especially vulnerable. Hard lessons are yet to be learned. The most brilliant and successful can have feet of clay.

Maybe just now, you are wrestling with such a situation. Blatant facts are there for others to inspect, but you keep insisting he or she should say it isn't so.

The human gods among us always fail sooner or later. Some do slowly and are barely noticed for a long time. Others seem to fall over a cliff with a terrifying thud. Regardless of the circumstances, the most significant thing we learn in such painful events is to never blindly trust in a person. All of us spiritually survive because of God's grace.

Fortunately, those who perceive they are seen in heroic light benefit from telling others they make mistakes — sometimes big ones. They do so humbly and sincerely.

Our God calls us to be genuinely good people. Those who are models for the young have a special responsibility. It helps to visualize little boys tearfully mumbling, "Say it isn't so."

"I will never be like her," she confidently emphasized. She was referring to her mother. At age eighteen, this daughter had already decided there were just too many things about her mother that she found inadequate.

For one thing, Mother did not treat her dad well. Even though he was a good man who paid a lot of attention to her, he was not given the credit due him. *She* would not make that mistake with her mate.

For another thing, Mother didn't understand that society needed an awful lot of changing. People Mother's age were missing so much by not making adjustments to today's living.

Time passed. The daughter went to college, graduated, and began a career. She married a fine, considerate, and loving man. Soon, she had two children of her own. They saw their grandmother occasionally, certainly not very often. In all this progression, the younger woman held to her intention of never being like her own mother.

Time continued to move quickly, and eventually her children graduated from college. Her mother was now in her seventies and it seemed only decent that the daughter spend more time with her. They talked, shopped, and cooked together. It was a wonderful time for her mother, who loved every moment they shared.

Her daughter began to wonder if they were alike in some ways. She looked in the mirror and saw a resemblance in their features and mannerisms. In fact, it soon became obvious that some of their thoughts ran along the same lines.

One day the daughter exclaimed to herself, "I have become like my mother!"

She admitted this to her mother and they both laughed. Her mother confided that she had the same experience with her own mother. Many of us are more like our parents than we admit.

62   Give Thanks for Differences

"They are all so different," two parents agreed. Father often chuckled and Mother would show concern. They were talking again about their four children, now in their thirties and forties. One son became a computer analyst and the other a brick mason. Indeed, they were different!

One daughter became a beautician and the other a veterinarian. To look at them and know them, one would never guess they were sisters.

Dad went on chuckling and Mom couldn't help worrying. In her opinion, it seemed a lot better to be a brick mason and live near your parents. Traveling all over the country with that computer stuff worried her.

Yes, and what about more grandchildren? The beautician had a son and the vet had no children, even though she had been married well over ten years.

As the generations come and go, most of us have dealt with these differences. With all the opportunity and movement in the last thirty years, such conflicts and variations arise. Most of us couldn't even imagine this years ago.

Of course, even years ago, we saw big differences among brothers and sisters. Not everyone wanted to work on the family farm or in the local factory.

My parents had three sons. One, Joe, became a career officer in the army and flew helicopters. Another, Mike, spent more than forty working years as a successful labor leader.

Well, many of you know something about me, and can see by comparing and contrasting that there are major differences in our family's path. This always seemed to me to be something to celebrate.

How about you? Do you give all your children credit for who and what they are, plus the vocations they have chosen? The black sheep may not be one at all.

Oh yes, we all have our problems. Some of us have not turned out the way our parents wanted, but unless there are serious moral or criminal issues, give thanks.

Keep on loving each and every one of them. It just might be better to chuckle with dad than worry with mom.

As parents, if we have kept our prayers up-to-date for our children, then God is in charge. And frankly, there's no better solution than that.

63 Self-Congratulations Can Cripple

"**H**appy for the wrong reasons," a smiling but stern grandmother related.

A recent happening in her grandson's life had produced her response. A personable young man, he was finishing high school with grades above average, and he had a bright future.

Yet, the young man was competitive and sometimes seemed like a general who followed the philosophy of "taking no prisoners." He wasn't quite vicious, in Grandmother's opinion, but she was nonetheless concerned.

The story—in brief—is that he wanted to be class president. Someone else aspired to the position, also, and worked very hard to get elected. At the last minute, however, the other candidate completely dropped out.

Grandson was unopposed and shared his happiness of being the new prexy. In fact, he arrogantly told others his competitor was afraid of him and didn't deserve the office anyway.

Grandson knew why the other fellow bowed out but never admitted it. The lad's parents were divorcing and he was devastated. It was a messy dissolution and very painful. The young man was hurt so badly that he nearly had a nervous breakdown.

Victorious Grandson went on his bragging ways. There was never an admission on his part of what really happened.

What disappointed Grandmother so much was that her grandson showed no compassion and respect for the other fellow. It was as though he had defeated some cowardly weakling.

When she saw her grandson, she praised his victory. But then she said, "Happy for the wrong reasons." She said she was ashamed he could be so happy and yet uncaring for a classmate who had a major misfortune.

She opened her well-worn Bible and read from Saint Paul's love chapter. "Love is not jealous or boastful; it is not arrogant or rude," she read carefully. He was an unwilling listener.

There was more. She emphasized, "Love does not rejoice in the wrong but rejoices in the right." Probably only Grandmother could deliver the needed message and she did splendidly.

He began to see the light. He didn't realize how totally absorbed he had been in his own interests and ambitions. Is there a lesson here for you and me to meditate upon?

64   The Media and Boredom

"Isn't there something new?" she inquired, watching the evening news on TV. Very sensitive to the world around her, she loved life with its challenges and surprises.

She was a professional woman, well educated and doing well in a managerial position. She was unmarried and had no plans to be otherwise, so much of her free time was spent enjoying the media.

But she noticed a change occurring. Life had become the "same old, same old." She sought for newness, and discovered even highly recommended movies and shows evidenced more sameness.

Boredom had rarely bothered her, but now she was experiencing it more often.

Her health was excellent, money was more than adequate, a few friends were good to her, and job security was okay. Was age the problem? She had just passed thirty-five. What was wrong?

She began to analyze her life and its experiences. At first she blamed herself. Then — in time — something became quite obvious and she was grateful.

The lack of newness was not her or any slippage in her intellectual powers. She observed a reality other sharp persons were also experiencing, especially from the media circus.

The media orchestrated an unending commentary on everything. She had begun to say to herself, *Who cares?* She wasn't alone in her realization of media overload.

The media culture was packed with the tired, sordid, miscellaneous, and unprofitable. It was like some telephone conversation that began and ended the same way, with little in between.

It seemed so much was framed in the same old point of view, often a matter of the so-called liberal versus conservative. Even columnists were known decidedly to be one or the other.

Who was doing open creative thinking, refusing to grind axes in favor or against something? Who was willing to take some tried-and-true basics of living and speak of them in experiential ways?

She was. She went on her weekly trip to the local bookstore. For the first time in a long time, she spent three hours in the religion section. She came across an incredible book.

The discerning woman bought three copies of *The Imitation of Christ* by Thomas á Kempis, one to study and two to give away. Its opening line quoted John's Gospel: "No follower of mine shall ever walk in darkness."

65   Enabling Sincere People

"**C**ut the nonsense," said the successful executive. He was effective and competent, he applied his art.

Some, perhaps more crudely, would use the term *crap* rather than *nonsense*. However we say it, the reality is clear. In today's world, many deal with endless, seemingly unnecessary barriers to achieving anything, be it talking to the banker or ordering a pizza.

Call it red tape or any color you select. Sometimes, precious hours and even days are wasted in sorting through options. While we don't want to be unnecessarily unfair with the health care industry, it seems that's one area where many have all had such bad experiences. When we attempt to get through on the phone, why do we have to listen to seemingly endless menus? But let's not slight other institutions and organizations. It goes on many places, doesn't it? Maybe we are not actually cutting through the nonsense, we are just biding our valuable time until a live body answers.

Those of us who have lived most of our lives on schedules, by appointment, and with an eye on the clock can also be impatient. Yet without being no nonsense and straight to the point, how else can we serve people efficiently?

As we seek to adjust to an even more complicated world, we need to be aware there are truly good people caught up in the system who want to be helpful. People want to do their jobs and do them well. They care about others and want to do an honest day's work; unfortunately, they often end up in failure.

What does the Christian faith say about this? While we cannot return to the days of walking with Jesus and the apostles along the Sea of Galilee, we can do something else.

For example, only recently I spent hours trying to get through barriers and barricades over the phone in regard to a specific situation. Finally, I got into the car and drove a few miles to an office. There I discovered a deeply frustrated lady.

She sat behind her desk with the phone to her ear, trying to take notes. She looked dejected, alone, and exhausted. The whole system had dumped on her.

For a brief moment, we visited. I assured her she was appreciated, all that went wrong wasn't her fault, and God really cared. When I left, she smiled and thanked me.

66 Unwanted Gifts

"You snooze, you lose," the ambitious young fellow said almost defiantly. He had just gotten out of college and this would be his motto for his life.

In high school and college, he had been competitive, sometimes bordering on vicious. He was the kind of guy who was put down only temporarily. He always got up.

His admirers were many but so were his detractors. His philosophy of life was really quite simple: One should never be asleep to the slightest opportunity.

Friends came and went. Most everything he touched was successful. He applied his favorite phrase. Fairly soon he became known far and wide for his successes.

While not an immoral or irreligious man, he sometimes used certain infractions by people around him to further his agenda. That seemed only natural.

As he approached his thirty-fifth birthday, an upstanding and spirit-filled evangelist told him the Lord had a gift for him. That sounded a lot like proverbial poppycock to the ambitious man.

God is great, but gifts came by being fully alert to one's talents and energies for succeeding, the man avowed. In a way he was saying if God wouldn't bother him, he wouldn't bother God! Nothing was to get in the way of successful personal fulfillment.

Then a routine annual trip to the physician's office found the beginning of colon cancer. Convinced that was most likely a mistake, he sought a second opinion.

This opinion confirmed the first and with more credence. He had to take some days off for his surgery; for the first time in his life, he was going to be required to "snooze."

At first, he thought his schedule could not be interrupted, but as the pain and bleeding increased, he knew something had to be done.

The surgery was lengthy and very complicated. Days and weeks passed. One day, a nurse came by with a hand-written note from the evangelist. It simply said, "Wait on the Lord and be satisfied." The gift was given.

As he wept, it was obvious a conversion experience was occurring. When he eventually recovered, even his enemies were impressed by his now radically altered life philosophy.

"Love is not enough," she pointedly told her husband. Well, he had always been a romantic and very respectful kind of guy, but she had become more distant and less interested in going the usual places with him. Concern soon gripped him.

After a period, he risked confronting her. He asked her if some other man was in her life. She cried and yet could understand his inquiry. She assured him the only other man in her life was their son.

Was she telling the truth? He did some probing here and there, feeling guilty all the time but wanting to know the truth. Nothing—absolutely nothing—turned up and he was relieved.

What was the matter? People marveled at their marriage; their children were delightful and smart. Weren't they just as much in love as they were twenty years ago as high school sweethearts? He was even more in love with his wife than ever before.

He came home every night, almost always on time. He was generous with his paycheck, letting her spend most of it. Her husband felt happy and secure.

She, however, had expected more socializing and more luxury in their marriage. As they neared middle age, her love was starting to be strained. She needed to get out and socialize with others. She had always wanted to travel, too.

Her husband was a homebody, though. His income had never allowed them to move from their modest but comfortable home. He had felt no need to seek promotions or change jobs.

Must two fine people—husband and wife—drift apart because a love once satisfying has diminished or changed on her part?

Strong needs never met will eventually cry out to be satisfied. We forget that romantic love has its limits. We also tend to forget human love never has the depth and breadth of God's love.

But there is a solution. Together, the two must explore the unhappiness; with patience, perseverance, trust, and compromise, they will—with God's help—find a way to meet in the middle.

68   A Miraculous Mystery

"I tried so hard," he kept lamenting at the water's edge. Medical school had turned him down again. Everything he knew said now he could not get in at all.

The lake's waters were deep and he was alone, except for a few birds in the nearby trees. His hope had reached an all-time low.

His anxiety level was so high he was partly disoriented. He was ready to flip a coin to see if he should jump into the inviting waters, ending it all there and then.

All he ever really wanted to be was a physician. Being a specialist with a widely-known reputation was of no interest. He simply wanted to be a medical doctor to and for others.

As you might guess, he was so angry at God that he thought hell might claim him at any moment. He experienced no mercy in all of this and eventually proceeded to shout at his Creator.

He was married to a lovely young woman, a professional in her own right. She continually encouraged him. Children had been delayed until he could finish med school. She didn't know where he was and waited in their apartment for his return.

It seemed he had stayed at the water's edge for an eternity. Daylight mattered very little and the playful frogs even less. Could there possibly be a way out of this?

In his despair, he decided to tie a heavy piece of cement to his body and wade into the lake. Then, as the water reached his neck, he would simply lay down in his watery grave. At that point, he would not be able to get up and his failure soon would be a part of the lake's forgotten debris. He told himself over and over that he deserved death, and he began to look forward to being no more.

Can someone hate himself or herself that much? Well, the answer is in the affirmative. And what of God? In such torment, it may seem as though God no longer loves, is devoid of mercy, and frankly, could care less.

But that's not the truth. The young man didn't go through with it, and for a remarkable reason. As he stood by the lake, a fisherman came by and said, "Please give me your raging anger and heavy cement." Then, he said, "My life has been lived and I will die in your place, so you might have another chance at life."

69   Encourage One Another

"You can do it!" the young and vivacious woman called out. It was one of her favorite expressions. She loved saying it; the words always seemed to energize her. She was excited about life. There was happiness about her that inspired others. If only the world could capture it.

As she watched a runner labor to the finish line, she would boldly encourage him to go for it, even if he were already out of the race.

Once, she observed an old fellow trying to ride a bicycle down the block. He wasn't doing very well at all but she cheered him on with gusto.

One day she watched a woman try to push her lifeless car across an intersection. Do you know what happened? Ms. Positive Plus kept telling her she could do it, and she did.

People like her are the cheerleaders of humanity. Anything can be conquered.

I wish we could grow more people like this. Their win-win attitudes enhance all of us and we all turn out to be better people because of them.

We were not put upon this earth to fail; we were put here for accomplishment. Success means taking others with us.

This young woman's style is like a trumpet sounding an angelic invitation to the cause of human betterment. Granted, this isn't heavy theology, but it works wonders.

Obviously, we won't always succeed, but it's great to know that someone genuinely believes in you and wants to cheer you on.

70 Talent May Be Little Appreciated

"**P**lease recognize my work," he cried out in sorrowful tones. The fellow made a living at the local factory, but that was not his first love. His passion was art; he drew sketches by the hundreds.

Occasionally, he'd enter one or more in a contest, but they never received an award. Viewers and judges didn't criticize his work—they just did not seriously consider it.

He was a quiet and conservative man who lived alone. Being famous or even infamous was never his goal. He had all the money he needed, so prize money was of no consequence.

What he wanted more than anything else was to be recognized for making a contribution to life. People didn't even need to tell him he was gifted.

He felt it was his sketches that mattered. He saw himself as someone whose talent could enhance people's lives. He desired recognition for his work, not himself.

In my pilgrimage among and with people, I have found very few like that! Who among us is ready to say, "I don't want fanfare or even recognition for myself, but please recognize my work?"

If we get our pictures in the papers, are interviewed on TV, or speak to top organizations—to many, that's what matters. Our work may be little more than a tool that enables us to be temporarily seen.

His sketches were of quality and unique. No one ever said that to him and his pain stemmed from this oversight. He yearned for others to appreciate his contribution. His wait was long and the torment in his soul produced a most unhappy human being.

He didn't indicate to others that he felt it was time his sketches were given proper recognition. That would compromise him in a way he would have found totally unacceptable.

Often we have trouble pointing out other people's gifts. Is it a matter of jealousy or simply not wanting to take the time? Think on that, privately and slowly. Acknowledging someone's gifts—celebrating someone's work—can change their life for the better.

71   What We Sow, We Reap

"I wish it were not true," an aged gentleman said sadly and with a deep frown. He had lived many years and had known many crises, but this time, it was all he could handle and then some.

His nearly sixty-year-old son was dead. His death was tragically public and caused great pain to many. In his death, virtually all the good of his life was cancelled.

I guess we have all known those situations. Sometimes entire communities seem to scratch their heads in disbelief, and among the deceased's special friends, denial is much in the air.

In this case, an upright and seemingly moral son made a serious mistake. The president of a bank, he had deliberately manipulated records to increase his personal fortune.

When it came to light, hardly anyone believed it. It was so in opposition to everything that made him a pillar in the community. Years of apparent integrity had built the bank.

Yet he was guilty. The money had gone for gambling, personal travel, and women.

No one had suspected him. He had been a highly respected elder in his church and his credibility was probably the highest of almost anyone in the area.

The tragedy was greatly compounded by the way he chose to die. On Friday, when the bank was crowded, he put a revolver to his head with his office door open and took his own life.

There were screams and scrambling about. Not a soul in the bank that day would ever forget the experience. Anger and pity encompassed those present. Real compassion was hard to find.

For his father, incapacitated in a nursing home in his early nineties, it was like dying with a broken heart.

Even in this terrible event, there is a key lesson to learn. Everyone—except One—has the potential to disappoint us . . . tragically.

The words of Jesus are there for all of us to see and believe. He tells us, "I will never leave you nor forsake you." He is the only one you can fully count on.

"Oh, just reminiscing," she said, a rather angelic look on her face. Beautiful memories flooded her consciousness, giving her a sense of peace and fulfillment.

She wasn't quite eighty years of age yet, but now for some time, especially with her husband gone, she reminisced. Occasionally, something or someone would come across her mental screen that made her frown. Yes, and there were times she shed tears of hurt and regret. But for the most part, her reminisces brought her pleasure.

Some people have a streak of sentimentality that grows stronger as they grow older. Hours can be spent remembering and interpreting.

Many churches have a large number of seniors who are past-oriented. Some have a way of reminiscing that is like catching a wonderful disease!

I plead guilty. The great preponderance of happenings in my life have been positive and growth producing. So many have given so much to this seventy-year-old man.

Just the other day, I visited the Cooper Science Building at Ball State. I found dozens of pictures of graduating nurses on one of the walls.

I latched onto the class of 1937, and there, pert and pretty, was my Aunt Erma Lacy, later Kleihauer. A real knockout, she was also the president of her class.

To my knowledge, she was the first to graduate in my family with a degree beyond high school. Later she married a Methodist minister in Chicago and they reared a lovely family.

But thinking of Aunt Erma is more than just a reminiscence. The exercise powerfully brought my whole life together.

So much of who and what we are comes from those who have touched our lives. I would dare not try to list all that have influenced mine—there are just so many!

I will say, and admit gratefully, that Erma's husband, Hopkins, was a chief reason I have been a Methodist pastor these many years. He gave this small town boy a new way of looking at the world.

Be grateful as you recount past experiences. Even if pain and hurt are in the picture, thank God for His love and mercy. I continue to thank Erma for the wise choice she made in choosing her mate.

73   Adultery's Many Casualties

"It was the aftermath that hurt," he said mournfully. His brother was in the hospital, not expected to live.

The story was long, complicated, and involved his brother's wife.

Unfaithfulness in marriage is not new, but it does seem our society has become more and more tolerant of it.

We live in a culture drenched by adultery. It's all over television, movies, books, and even the six o'clock news. Unfortunately, adultery is frequently treated as just another ailment that needs a bit of prescribed salve.

Across the country, how many pastors and counselors deal with people impacted by adultery? It has become more than an embarrassment. It is truly a national tragedy, sometimes treated with little real concern.

Until it happens to someone you know.

In this case, his brother's wife had forsaken her wedding vows. She admitted to the fact, but would not tell who her "friend" was. She never even hinted at his identity.

Their families were understanding and urged them to make peace by her admission and his forgiveness. Their teenage children pleaded, "Come on, Dad and Mom, this is over."

The husband agreed and life seemed to be capable of moving on. They would have some shaky times, but not to the point of separation and divorce. Loved ones breathed a sigh of relief.

Then, as the saying goes, "all hell broke loose." The man was identified—he owned up to the adulterous relationship—as a slightly older uncle of the husband. The affair had gone on for months unnoticed.

The betrayed husband jumped from an eight-story building, breaking or fracturing virtually every bone in his body. The brother stood by the bed and wept daily. Could hell be any worse?

The aftermath did hurt more than we can imagine. Adultery is always wrong. Flee from the slightest temptation.

74   No Substitute for Preparation

"**B**e well prepared," the wife told her husband in loving firmness. He was getting ready for a job interview for a position he had always wanted. Not only was the opportunity an increase in income, it would provide more time with his family and the promise of better use of his talents.

It's not always easy to prepare for something. There are often troublesome variables. We can be so nervous that we are close to a breakdown!

Early in my ministry I can remember preparing carefully written sermons, using my experience as an English teacher. Every word had to have its proper place. No grammatical errors were allowed. I was really prepared. At least, I thought so. My congregation, except for a handful, gave mostly silent "ho hums," and talked about the weather.

The husband and father, on the other hand, was really prepared for this very promising job interview. He went to it confidently and in a spirit of letting God be the final determinant.

Everything went quite well. It was a long session because of the considerable responsibility involved. Interviewer and interviewee concluded on a highly satisfactory note.

His wife's advice was a big help. Like so many wives and mothers, she wanted all involved to benefit. Yes, and off the record, she just knew her man was the best one who applied.

In a few days, word came. He got the job.

The family celebrated by going to their favorite restaurant. It was a precious moment in their lives and God was indeed present.

There were still surprises coming. The position for which the man was hired was soon discontinued as unneeded.

Management drew up another job description, much more tailored to his talents and temperament. They said he was too big for the other position. The family settled in and praised God.

75   Growing Up Can Be Humbling

"**G**ive me a break!" the furious thirteen-year-old told his mother. The teenager's self-confidence was too high for his own good.

He thought his mother was cramping his style. Of course, he wanted to go out with the guys and show his prowess. Mom assured him he wasn't allowed to do that.

In today's world it seems that teenagers can get into more trouble in less time than teens of long ago.

The young teen wanted to spend the night at a cabin on a lake several miles from home. His friends were "nice" boys and they liked him a lot, he said. The problem seemed to be, as Mom pointed out, they were all older than he was. A couple of them had passed their eighteenth birthdays.

Later, when his mom was at work and his father was on the road with his job, he gave himself a break and took off with his friends.

The cabin was on a beautiful lake! It was the spring of the year and nature was doing her magnificent thing. The water was an exquisite blue, even inspirational. He was deliriously happy about it all.

As the afternoon became evening, the guys broke out alcoholic beverages. He wanted to belong so badly that he began to sample a bottle here and a can there. Before he knew it, he was feeling tipsy. Soon, the new teenager was having the time of his life (he thought) and was among friends (he thought).

But the others knew their limits and he didn't. They made him their favorite sport for the evening.

After some hours and a short trip to the water, the party was abruptly over. Not only was he very ill, he almost drowned.

At three o'clock in the morning he sat on a rock, sobbing and scared.

On the way home, no one said much of anything. He had gotten his break and showed his mother he belonged with the guys. He walked into his home, fell into his mother's arms, and told her how much he loved her.

An Abundance of Bibles

"There is only one true Bible," the deacon proclaimed rather loudly. He and his church faced a fairly common problem. It was not a simple one and had to be taken seriously.

There were strong differences of opinion and it had to do with the bedrock of belief. Kindness seemed to be at a minimum.

The deacon said it was a sin to read and study anything other than the King James Version (KJV) of the Bible. He was quick to point out everyone should pray for Brother Jones and others. Brother Jones had been reading and studying several different Bibles. He enjoyed comparing and contrasting. In fact, he was thrilled by the ways of communicating God's Word.

With the great minds (and hearts) we have today, I believe we ought to do some sampling. Was the KJV used in the first century by the apostles and others? Of course not. It came into being hundreds of years later. The Holy Spirit, however, was much at work in that first century to ensure the validity of Holy Scripture.

The translations and revisions of the precious Word of God are a long and complicated story. To my knowledge, no published Bible dropped from the heavens, proclaiming to be the one and only.

As the centuries have passed, men and women under the inspiration of the Holy Spirit have preserved, protected, and passed on revelation.

How fortunate we are! Where would you and I be without the Holy Scriptures? Most likely in a society and culture permeated by atheism, paganism, and—at best—agnosticism.

When there is a problem such as this, tolerance must carry the day. With the truly inspiring Bible, why not let all versions speak to us? We may learn something new.

Our dear Lord says we are known by our love for one another. When we practice that very thing, the world is impressed. It is never impressed by our wrangling over matters that may not be important. Sometimes we just have to swallow our pride and admit God has sons and daughters who understand some things differently than we do. Read and study your Bibles carefully and devoutly . . . and let others do the same.

77 Cling to the Anchor of Christ

"Happy days are here again," she sang with much nostalgia. A whole series of events had gone her way. That hadn't happened for a long time, and indeed, it was most welcome.

The song came out of a period when new leadership in America came to power in 1933 and optimism was in the air; Grandmother just loved to talk about those days. It looked like the Great Depression would be over, and in a way, things did seem to be getting better in America.

Years later, the elderly lady just kept on singing the tune, and her children and little grandchildren listened. Her children had grown accustomed to her mood swings. When she was happy, everybody seemed happy.

The reverse was also true. Someone would say half in jest, "When Momma ain't happy, ain't nobody happy." Bless the dear lady's heart. She was on one of her roller coaster adventures again.

Medication helped some of the time, but the family knew she'd swung down into depression again.

Mood swings are common in today's culture. Many people are on top one day and at the bottom the next.

I believe all of us tend to go up and down the scale of mood changes. Many events and experiences press in upon us. We reach a saturation point.

Try to count the various stimuli that come upon you every day. While farm life of yesteryear was tough with much hard work, it was fairly simple. (Of course today's farming is very different.)

I believe some people are more impacted by depression than others. While I'm not a physician or an expert in this area, I have observed for many years an increase in extremes in people.

Could this be because they don't have an anchor in their souls? That sounds old-fashioned, but it's actually truth. When Jesus the Christ becomes the focus of one's entire life, many things change. Among them are moods, ideas, habits, and—most of all—behavioral patterns of stability.

When you turn the air blue at one moment and then become angelically serene the next, beware! You are adrift. Christ pleads, "Come unto Me" and be anchored.

78   Giving Help Requires Wisdom

"How can I help?" was her inquiry. She often approached others who seemed to be in need.

The lady often came to the aid of her friends, acquaintances, and even perfect strangers. She had a reputation for helpfulness that spread far and wide.

One day, a dignified-looking older gentleman, confined to a wheelchair in the local nursing home, caught her attention. He was trying to move about in his chair, not very successfully.

She offered her help. Could she move him to the other side of the room, where he could see TV better? Yes, she was told. Without hesitation, she did what he asked. Another good deed had been done.

Strangely, that did not turn out to be the case. He slumped down onto the floor and began complaining that she had abused him. She stood there dumfounded.

A nurse and an attendant came quickly to see what had happened. It was obvious he was very upset. He was gently questioned.

The lady was in shock. No one had ever accused her of anything. How on earth could she have abused him and why would he make such a scene that might tarnish her goodwill?

The staff was concerned because the gentleman had never responded in such a way before. They could count on his actions and reactions being above board. He was highly respected and coherent.

With further investigation, an explanation came out. The gentleman was very modest, especially around women. When the helpful woman moved him, a part of his lower body was exposed. When he attempted to cover himself, he slid out of the chair and to the floor. All of this embarrassed him and he overreacted. His own sense of well being was dependent on others seeing his body fully clothed.

In time, the lady and the modest fellow became friends. Both had learned a valuable lesson. For the first time, she sensed her vulnerability in giving. He learned a new reality of getting older.

In our often confused and violent world, unfortunately, we need to be somewhat on guard when we offer our services. I sincerely wish that was not the case, but it is. Always ask our Lord to be present, especially when offering your help to others.

"I can't hack it anymore," he called out, slumping over his desk. It was a moment he had hoped would never come. What would happen to his wife and family, plus others who counted on him?

He was forty-five years old and at the peak of his career. Employees were leaving the place he worked and more work was being placed on him to accomplish.

The job paid well and it was a key position in management. Over the years he had accumulated an excellent work record.

Why would his energy and focus be forsaking him now?

Little known to others, his heart had been bothering him. So far, the doctor had only issued a warning. Surgery was not planned and apparently all would be okay.

His biggest frustration was the fear of letting down those he loved. He had both a son and a daughter in college. He couldn't bear to have them drop out.

The thought occurred to him that maybe the most prudent thing to do was to keep on working with no thought of his lessened strength. If he died, his life insurance would be more than ample to provide for his family.

He prayed under his breath with total sincerity. God was close and he could sense that He heard every word. It was a precious and unique moment in his life because he rarely ever prayed.

A few tears dropped down his cheeks, and then he became stoic. He began once again to tackle his pile of work. The company's downsizing had turned an excellent employee into a person fighting for his life.

The decision was made to work on . . . regardless. He loved his family so much. There was too much at stake and he wanted no one to suffer because he had failed.

How does the story end? He died the next day at his desk.

It was a terribly sad day for his wife, family, and friends. What they didn't know was the day before, for the first time in his life, he had made peace with God.

80   Misreading the Signals

"Oh, she is stuck on herself," growled the fellow across the street. He had watched the woman come and go many times. She seldom ever looked his way and was always in a hurry.

For him, someone simply had to speak to him every time, or the person was "uppity" (or worse). He rated people that way. Not much else really mattered on his grading scale.

It never occurred to him that maybe the lady was timid or often very busy.

The truth was, rather than being stuck on herself, quite the reverse was true. She was often apprehensive she would do or say something that sent wrong signals. So she didn't speak to the man on the street.

Over a period of weeks and months, he formed an opinion of her—not at all positive. He criticized her to others. It had become a kind of mission for him. His attitude was such that the neighborhood picked up on it and some began to call her Miss Snooty.

Well, as is sometimes the case, he sneered at her once too often. She was a widow with grown children. Her son, a young fellow in his twenties, finally had enough.

So he paid a visit to Mr. Outgoing Personality. The young man really let him have it. Then, the son explained something.

Soon after his father had died, a man made acquaintance with his mother and sought to befriend her, or so she thought. She misread the situation and was raped in her own home.

After a lengthy period of recovery, she went out in public again. It took her months to even speak to a man, including those she knew.

Her critic put his head down and told the son what a miserable offender he was. Then, the two of them went to see his mother. The man got down on his knees and told her how sorry he was.

81 Giving Directions

"You can't get there from here," the sun-tanned elderly farmer said. How many times we have heard that expression? It punctuates the difficulty in giving directions.

Go two miles south, turn right, go to the big red barn on the left, and then go north a mile and a half. That's where you'll find your destination. Maybe.

Over the years, some of the finest people on the face of this earth have given me some of the most hilarious directions. While east-central Indiana is my home, I still have trouble discovering if I can "get there from here."

Lately, I hear about getting to a destination in terms of minutes, rather than a distance. I thought that was strictly big-city style, but now it seems others judge destinations by time, too.

How do you tell people how to get to where they say they want to go? Frankly, I feel like telling them to buy a map. I might even give them the money. It really would be simpler.

Of course, that would deprive all these people of a wonderful opportunity to interact with some wonderful locals.

For example, Charley relates the best way to get to the appliance store is to go by the old field house, to the second light, turn right at the mortuary, go five blocks, and look east.

Bill stipulates the way to the cleaners is to cross Washington Street, bear right to the limestone home, make a quick left, go two blocks, and it's the second business on the north side.

To say it's twelve minutes to a grocery store is to say little about directions. After all, that depends a lot on the speed and flow of traffic, doesn't it?

You see, I learned long ago that people have ways of giving directions that say a lot about who and what they are. Locals communicate when they give directions. They don't just get you to your destination, they let you know they have been here a while and know what they are talking about. In other words, they belong here. It's a good place to be.

People in a hurry, who mumble "so many minutes," don't really care about your intended destination. They just want to get rid of you. There is no time to visit.

I kind of like detailed directions and interaction. They help me appreciate where I'm going even more.

82   Modesty Is Always in Style

"All my friends have one," a teenage daughter stated in a matter-of-fact tone. Her mother didn't believe that. In fact, she knew some other mothers who would not be at all impressed with this swim suit.

It was really much less than conservative. Her mother considered it close to obscene. She was quick to point out all you had to do was blink your eye and you wouldn't see it, hardly even qualifying as a garment! Mom won this battle for the time being. It is safe to bet the whole war was not resolved.

Society seems to have revolution after revolution telling us what decency is. Even liberals sometimes shake their heads in dismay.

What does decency mean to you? Aren't there basic ways for gentlemen to behave? Likewise, aren't there basic ways for ladies to behave?

By definition, aren't ladies and gentlemen conservative, modest, and decent? Should wearing "barely there" swimming attire be considered ladylike?

I believe it's a matter of respect versus conformity. Respect was impressed upon earlier generations. Dressing like someone else was a secondary consideration. While we may have the freedom to do what we please, it certainly is not prudent to do so.

What some choose to wear for swimming is only a peek into a morality that has gone bankrupt. Remember that it isn't prudish to wear a decent-looking swimsuit.

83   What Does Your Resumé Say?

"Here is my resumé," he said, confidently and proudly. It was very impressive, listing two major college degrees and several years of excellent experience.

The potential employer was impressed. Everything seemed to be in order. He did not pick up any inconsistencies or anything that resembled exaggeration.

All references checked out and a contract was written.

The company was having to watch its salary allocations, so a final, more in-depth investigation was made. The university and each former employer were called.

The references were asked to give far more specific answers. This time, a five-minute phone call became fifteen. The results were surprising.

The university showed only one actual degree granted. The man had taken other courses, but they never led to a degree. Warning flags went up—quickly.

Former employers explained more in detail the real work history of the man. He was a strong starter but had trouble maintaining a high level of productivity. The references became somewhat defensive because they were all his close friends. Yet objectivity finally came to the surface.

It was obvious the resumé was seriously flawed.

The man wasn't hired. He was not who and what he said he was. The discrepancies were glaring. In fact, he was much less than who and what he claimed to be.

Is the resumé we put before others, not just prospective employers, accurate? Can we stand strong and healthy evaluation by others?

All of this leads me to wonder about the resumé I put before God. Am I that good? Have I been totally honest before Him and sought to be objective in all cases?

Fortunately, in spiritual matters God grants the grace necessary to be made right with Him, regardless of our resumés. He has a perfect way of telling us who and what we are.

84   **Sometimes Secrecy Is Best**

"I accept you just the way you are," the clergyman emphatically stated. He was speaking to a parishioner in trouble with the church.

Although no one really knew the truth yet, some were gossiping.

He had been very active in the church, holding different positions. Now he was sinking lower and lower, even finding it difficult to attend services.

So the pastor asked him to come by his study for a visit. The pastor affirmed the parishioner in words of full acceptance. The man just sat there with his head down, so the pastor repeated the words.

He then looked up with tears in his eyes and began to unload his heavy burden. No on else had heard this confidential account. The air was heavy, the pain was obvious, and the humiliation was great.

He had stolen from his brothers and sisters in Christ. He was guilty of taking money from the church. Since he regularly helped count Sunday offerings, he'd had the opportunity. He had taken money on several occasions.

It had escaped people's attention until recent weeks. Someone wrote an anonymous note.

Since many gave only cash and wanted no credit for their giving, it had been a dream situation for the man. He admitted taking cash that exceeded a thousand dollars.

By way of restitution, the pastor and the parishioner agreed that twice the amount taken would find its way into the offering plates over a period of time. He would be able to privately correct what he had done. Why? Because the pastor in Christlike love had affirmed him as a precious human being.

85   More Patience, Lord

"I have this wonderful deal for you," the voice said over the phone. Well, to be honest, these may not have been the exact words, yet the telemarketer's intent was obvious.

I wonder how many more tremendous deals I am going to be called about. Day and night, they keep coming. There never seems to be a let-up. Boy, are some of these people shrewd! They must be carefully trained with all the latest psychological data. I do believe some could sell ice cubes to Eskimos.

I'd like to think I am always kind and considerate. I'd like to think I never want to tell them to go to an awful place. Yes, and I'd like to think I never slam the phone down.

Well, by now, you know my feelings and some of my reactions. The truth of the matter is, I should call back and say I am sorry. I haven't done that yet.

There is a magnificent book entitled *The Imitation of Christ* that often teaches things I would rather not be taught. One of them is about patience. Talk about dynamite!

The book says, in essence, don't try to choose the people or situations you want to teach you patience. God has His plan. Don't try to manipulate things to your liking and tastes.

Doggone it, I don't want to learn patience from telemarketers, Lord. It is beneath me. I am a man of clergy and really need something more befitting.

Wouldn't you think the dear Lord would choose a more appropriate lesson giver? *After all, I know from whom and what I need to learn. Why doesn't He recognize that?*

Spiritual growth ought to be neat and tidy. Patience should be learned from those we know, respect, and like. They will help us, love us, and above all forgive us.

As you can tell, I am still trying to learn patience. Golly, some days it is hard! Some days I can hear the Almighty God of the universe say bluntly, "Don, pay attention." I need to bury my pride and stop fighting Him.

Okay, telemarketers, hit me again. I mean, *call* me again. I promise to behave myself and be a Christian gentleman. *Dear God, can't you make it a little easier?*

Affluence Isn't All It's Cracked Up To Be

"We are too bloated with things," a Sunday school teacher told her students. She had lived beyond eighty and remembered the Great Depression very vividly.

Her students thought she must be coming out of ancient times. After all, aren't things what life is all about? Someone has flippantly said whoever has the most toys at the end wins.

When she spoke of wasting food, they thought she must be out of touch. She got quite specific with her questions. "Why did you throw away that beautiful sausage at Bob Evans?"

She went on with her questions. They weren't quite sure whether they were bored or just uncomfortable. After all, wasn't it their right to throw away food they didn't want?

"Why did you take one bite off that sumptuous chicken leg and toss it in the garbage heap?" "So, you don't care much for green beans? Suppose you only had green beans to eat?"

She talked about the times her father could only put certain things on their table. For one meal they had potatoes and corn. Then for the next meal, corn and potatoes.

Her mother worked so hard to prepare the food. Her father was embarrassed because he just couldn't provide anything else. She remembered her mother's tears and the pain in her father's face.

It was probably harder on her father. In those days, a man's worth was solidly tied to what he could give to his family.

The end of the session found most of the youth very quiet. The unspoken words were more potent than what was being said. "You mean it really was that way back then?"

"Gosh, is it possible we are too bloated with things?" "Yes, and am I as wasteful as she seems to think? Yet doesn't God want me to have a good time and feel good?"

"Johnny, eat everything on your plate before you get up to go play." "Susie, the pork chops are there to be eaten; we only throw away the bones." Maybe this is just old-fashioned stuff.

That wonderful old lady came out of a different period of history. She doesn't want her students to live the way she did, but she wants them to appreciate what they have.

Regardless of your age, God's goodness calls for grateful and intelligent response.

87   Called to Live and Let Live

"How can I be sure?" she said emotionally. She couldn't help it. The important inquiry was imbedded in her heart and mind.

It had to do with stories told in whispers about her mother and father. She was well beyond the age of twenty-one, but that did not stop her questioning. Was her dad really her biological father?

Both of her parents had assured and reassured her for years. Yet, there were the whispers and this lingering tug inside of her. Sometimes it virtually haunted her.

It was like an ongoing aching that never stopped. Oh, it would subside from time to time, but rarely did it leave her for very long.

Was there any way she could be sure one way or another? There was testing that could be done, provided she could get her parents' cooperation. She knew they wouldn't, however.

So, the gnawing continued, even though she kept telling herself not to be so anxious. Her parents had tried to persuade her for years just to take their word. No solution.

We have all been there, haven't we? Our matters and issues may be different, but we still can't help wondering about something. My guess is anyone over thirty has experienced this, maybe more than once.

Such pain is real and not imagined. For a sensitive person, it can lead to mental and emotional imbalance. For the strict moralist, it can be a very heavy cross to bear.

As a pastor, I have tried to get people to be totally honest, and at the same time, forgiving. We are called to forgive.

Total honesty and total forgiveness in the long run lead to healing. If her dad isn't her biological father, she needs to know that, but also to give the necessary forgiveness. To be told a blatant lie over and over is usually harder on the liar than anyone else. Truth and forgiveness would free them all. Also knowing why the lie was perpetuated might aid in that release.

In our lives, we cannot always be sure of people. One person we can be sure of is Jesus, who says He is the Way, the Truth, and the Life.

88   May God Be Merciful

"Talented and attractive" was how people always described her. She was one of those unusual young women who seemed to have it all at an early age. Others were amazed by her gifts.

In both college and graduate school she excelled, catching the eyes of virtually everyone. What promise she offered in any career she chose!

She rose rapidly in the ranks of the business world. Men seemed to be standing in line for her recognition, whether it be for professional or romantic reasons.

She had made a decision on her thirtieth birthday, however, that she would neither marry nor have children under any circumstances. Men could come and go in her life, but she refused to let them interfere in her wonderful career.

Everyone marveled at her huge successes. Corporations sought both her talent and attractiveness. She would never give up the thrill and affirmation of those who practically worshiped her success.

Through the years men would come and go in her life, but she kept on the same career path. Then a careful look in the mirror one day frightened her.

A promiscuous personal life had begun to take its toll. She sought a better hair dresser, manicurist, and pedicurist. She also began dieting and exercising more.

Things moved along smoothly again for a time, and the mirror was either avoided or discounted. Eventually, she began to notice that some people, especially her competition, looked at her differently.

At the age of forty-seven, something happened. A routine physical exam found cancer on the rampage in her body. At first, she viewed it as just something else to overcome and move on.

She was determined that her talents and attractiveness would continue to shine. Every effort was made to see this happen, including borrowing money for the most expensive physicians and hospitals.

Confined to a hospital bed, her attitude remained the same: "This too shall pass and in time the world will again marvel at me and my successes." Despite all money could buy, this was not to be.

She fell into a coma and no one could converse with her. Death was near. She and she alone would hear a still, small voice say, "This night your soul is required of you."

All Christians Are in Sales

"**Y**ou name it, I got it," the salesman said with a ring of credibility and genuineness.

He was very successful and could deliver the goods. He rarely had a disappointed customer. His reputation was known far and wide, even across economic and social boundaries.

The thought occurs to me that we should be like that in our religious lives. If the name of Jesus is mentioned, do we have Him? In other words, can we deliver?

It is a sad state of affairs to proclaim the faith and then be unable to deliver it. Faith and works do go hand in hand. You really can't have one without the other.

To profess the Christian religion is to say, in essence, "I know what this is about and can tell you." We are supposed to be able to deliver the goods. We should be able to share the Lord.

A man told me long ago that pastors are always in sales. Every morning when they get up, they hit the floor selling others. I didn't like that idea at the time, but the truth of the matter is we are all in sales, whether laity or clergy.

Most of the selling is done without words. Our attitudes and behavior make or break us in sales. A brilliant sermon by someone who does not practice what they preach seriously cripples the whole operation.

Perhaps the worst mistake we could make, however, is to argue. I have never known a successful salesman whose strategy involved arguing. They were all clear, quick, and positive.

That's a good blueprint for all of us in sales for Christ. Be clear, quick, and positive. That's the way we get the job done of Christ and His Church.

We should tell the story that we know deep within us, using clarity, quickness, and positive language. Never belabor, argue, or be negative.

So much is at stake in the kind of selling we do — it has eternal repercussions.

90   Someone Who Cares

"**D**oesn't anybody care?" she asked with tears streaming down her cheeks. Her physician told her she had cancer and it was bad.

At the age of forty, this news broke her heart and left her broken. So, she spoke the only words that came to her. She felt alone, and all at once no one cared.

So much had been right about her life. She had three lovely and well-behaved children, and a good husband for eighteen years, who loved her and the children.

Yet, all that seemed to make any sense to her was her cry for somebody to care. It is a sad scene and one filled with questions. Surely the physician was wrong.

The truth of the matter is he was not wrong. Her days to live were measured in a number of weeks. It was time to prepare a funeral for someone who had lived only half of her life.

Of course, there were people who cared. It was more than lip service; they really did care. But she couldn't feel any of that at the moment, and the tears flowed.

Our tendency may be to be very sympathetic and then gently scold her for asking the question. "Surely, dear, you know there are people who care. They are all about you and will love you."

But wait a minute. Have you and I been there, knowing the moment our death was pronounced with many planned years left? Have we been there and done that, as the saying goes? We don't know what she's experiencing.

She is experiencing alienation and even betrayal. She feels God must have forsaken her and no longer cares, either, even though her life has been lived with few blemishes (none of any consequence).

Maybe it's time for us to remember those sad words of Jesus: "My God, my God, why have You forsaken me?" These are perhaps the most strange words in the Scriptures. Why, Lord, why?

He was perfect in every way. Yet He sensed an alienation so painful it is hard for us to understand, except as we experience something similar. This dear lady teaches us a lesson.

Unless you and I have been there and done that, the least said the better. When we have been there, most likely there will be no scolding. There may very well be serious silent prayer.

Those who suffer teach us much. To suffer is to be in fellowship with Jesus and experience the reality of the nail prints. There may be no other way to find Him and serve Him.

91   God Has the Last Word

"There is some good in everyone," his mother often said with authority. As a child, he believed what she said. He felt no need to test its veracity.

By the time he graduated from high school, he had really begun to wonder, and doubts arose. Was Mom right?

He had learned about the activities of Adolph Hitler, Joseph Stalin, Saddam Hussein, several serial killers, and many others. It no longer seemed that her teaching on this matter would hold up.

In college, the issue seemed to cross his mind almost every day. The young man pondered. He kept thinking about it largely because his mother had planted the seed so early.

In a quiet moment one day, God came to him in that "still, small voice."

He knew he was on the verge of a career change from business to the ordained ministry. God had drawn him.

He felt called to deal with the goodness of humankind. He had to find out if those who had done really bad things had any hope of salvation. He cared deeply about this.

His answer came in Matthew 6:14–15, which deals with forgiving others and God forgiving you. It also deals with not forgiving others and God not forgiving you. He was both thrilled and frightened by this passage.

It was then that he knew his mother was at least partially right. God is good and He created all of us. If all people deserve forgiveness, then there has to be some spark of goodness in everyone.

This stayed with him on the battlefields in human relations in his churches. Forgiveness for all—even those who might try to destroy him—would not be optional. It would be an ongoing necessity.

About the Author

As a United Methodist pastor and published writer for almost fifty years, Donald Charles Lacy has traveled many stimulating and enriching roads.

He earned bachelor of science and master of arts degrees from Ball State University. He received a master's and a doctorate from Christian Theological Seminary.

Lacy has pastored churches across the state of Indiana and published well over one thousand pieces that have included books, newspaper columns, magazine features, book reviews, devotionals, and liturgies. A representative sampling of his published material appears in his *Collected Works* (Providence House Publishers, 2001).

Lacy is nationally known for his commitment to Christian unity between both Protestants and Catholics. In an interview about Mary, the mother of Jesus, he is pictured in the March 21, 2005 issue of *Time* magazine.

Donald Charles Lacy and his wife, Dorothy, reside in Muncie, Indiana, and have four daughters and two grandchildren.